OREGON

LAKE MAPS

&

FISHING GUIDE

FAP

Frank Amato
Publications

OREGON
LAKE MAPS &
FISHING GUIDE

Note: Numbers refer to detailed maps inside

Contents

IMPORTANT CONTACT INFORMATION

- **Oregon Department of Fish and Wildlife,** (503) 947-6000 or (800) 720-6339, www.dfw.state.or.us
- **United States Coast Guard, Emergencies:** Dial 911 or call the Coast Guard on Marine Channel 16, www.uscg.mil/d13/msuportland
- **Tide Chart,** www.or.usharbors.com/monthly-tides
- **Oregon State Parks,** (503) 986-0707, **Reservations:** (800) 452-5687, **Information:** (800) 551-6949, www.oregonstateparks.org
- **US Forest Service,** www.fs.fed.us/recreation
- **Oregon Bureau of Land Management,** (503) 375-5646, www.blm.gov/or
- **U.S. Bureau of Land Management,** www.blm.gov/or
- **Oregon Department of Forestry,** www.odf.state.or.us
- **Turn In Poachers, Oregon Program,** (800) 452-7888
- **Oregon State Park Reservations,** www.reserveamerica.com

- **Oregon State Parks,** www.stateparks.com
- **Guide to Oregon's Central Coast,** www.newportnet.com
- **Boat Escape: Oregon's Ultimate Boating Resource,** www.boatescape.com
- **Oregon Parks Association,** www.orparks.org
- **RV Park Finder,** www.rvparkfinder.net
- **Oregon Fishing Guides Organization,** www.oregonfishingguides.org
- **Oregon Shellfish Areas,** www.dfw.state.or.us/mrp/shellfish
- **Oregon Fly Fishing,** www.oregononthefly.com
- **Northwest Fly Fishing,** www.west-fly-fishing.com
- **Oregon Fly Fishing Shops,** www.askaboutflyfishing.com
- **RV Park Reviews,** www.rvparkreviews.com/regions/oregon
- **Southern Oregon Fishing,** www.southernoregonfishingreports.com

WARNING!
IMPORTANT NOTICES

Boating: This book is not meant for navigational purposes. Before proceeding down any river or stretch of river, boaters should visually check the water first. It should be remembered that all the rivers in this book are subject to floods and high water and their currents and courses change frequently. Extreme caution is advised at all times, as is the use of Coast Guard-approved personal floatation devices (pfds).

Fishing Regulations: Fishing regulations often change, especially due to the complexities of managing steelhead and salmon populations. Check the Oregon Sport-Fishing Regulations booklet before each season, and before fishing a new piece of water.

Editor: Gary Lewis • **Book Design & Maps:** Esther Poleo-Appel Design, 503-641-8079

Cover Photo: Patrick Clayton • **Photography:** Gary Lewis, Jim Schollmeyer and Dave Hughes

Illustrations: Dürten Kampmann and Jesse Sandberg

Frank Amato Publications

All inquiries should be addressed to:

PO Box 82112 • Portland, Oregon 97282 • (503) 653-8108

Softbound ISBN-13: 978-1-57188-517-3 • Softbound ISBN-10: 1-57188-517-X • UPC: 0-81127-00368-6

Printed in China

©2014 Frank Amato Publications, Inc.

INTRODUCTION

There is only one right way to start a where-to-go-fishing book. You have to go fishing.

This project kicked off with a trip to Lake Billy Chinook for bull trout with my friend Brett Dennis. We fast-stripped lead-head minnow imitations. The fish averaged 17 inches and when they grabbed, it was electric. A few days later, we fished Davis Lake with Howard Abshere, where five-pound largemouth bass hammered our ten-inch bullet-head Bunny Leeches.

The fastest day of fishing was a Sunday in July at Anthony Lake in northeast Oregon, when in two hours, I had over 100 grabs and landed 23 trout. One trout for every 5.2 minutes. Toward the end of that stretch, I tied up a tandem rig with a French Pheasant Tail and a Zug Bug and caught two fish on one cast.

By the third week of July, East Lake was fishing very good. We hit the water with Scott Cook early in the morning and landed Atlantic salmon, kokanee, and over a dozen rainbows each. We kept hoping to hook a brown, but the East Lake Grand Slam eluded us that day.

My dad and I had a good day at North Fork Reservoir on the upper Clackamas one evening in September. Instead of pulling flies, we trolled Ford Fenders with tiny Dick Nite spoons. The slower we trolled, the faster the fish grabbed.

We saved some of the best water for September and October. Fred Foissett and Ryan Young helped me ring in autumn at Lava Lake, where fat rainbows slammed our rusty brown and olive leeches.

Once, while traveling with my family, our paths crossed with the King of Jordan and the Prince staying at the Rogue Regency in Medford. But there was no time for hobnobbing with royalty, there were fish to catch.

One of the most difficult aspects of writing the **Oregon Lake Maps & Fishing Guide** was picking water. Oregon isn't the land of Ten Thousand Lakes, but it is the land of a whole lot of good fishing lakes and reservoirs. There are guide books that document almost all of Oregon's fishing water and the best waters of parts of the state. But there is no fishing guide like this one, that explains the top 40 best lakes and reservoirs, charts the best fishing times, maps fishing locations and connects you with guides, tackle shops, lodging and local information.

Chances are that you have already looked at the Table of Contents. Maybe your home water is documented. Maybe it's not. In picking lakes, we broke the state into regions, then identified the most important fishing stillwaters or the water that was representative of other lakes and reservoirs in the vicinity. The intent was to provide a visual representation to give you, the angler, a place to start when trying someplace new.

One of the challenges, especially when fishing new water, was to learn to read it quickly. Every lake has its own dynamic. It helped, when fishing a lake for the first time, or the first time in a long time, to talk to lodge operators, store employees and other fishermen. Fishing connects people from all different walks of life. It was heartwarming and inspiring to meet and make new friends in every corner of the state. And we enjoyed good days on the water.

READING WATER

One of the best skills the traveling angler can develop is the ability to 'read' the water. It is not as easy on a lake or a reservoir as it is on creek and river.

After the new fisherman learns to cast and present bait, lure, or fly, the next lesson is on reading water. "Look for the pockets, fish the seams," the teacher counsels. The student learns to catch trout in rivers and becomes enamored with moving water.

Years later, the neophyte has become master of the methods that take fish on streams both large and small. But he trembles when he considers fishing still water. Lakes and the fish that inhabit them are intimidating. Many veteran anglers stay away because they have never learned how to read lakes and reservoirs.

The rewards are great. Trout in food-rich lakes have the potential to grow far bigger than their stream-bound cousins. In a lake, small trout can put on pounds without a daily workout.

What you see on the surface is like the cover of a book. It doesn't tell the whole story, but the picture hints at the contents. Where a ridgeline runs down to the surface, it most likely continues below; where a beach slopes gently to water, expect the shallows to extend a longer distance. Perhaps weed growth has worked its way to the top. Weeds provide habitat for insects and minnows and the predators that feed on them.

Where Does an Angler Start?

The two most important considerations are depth of the water and the temperature. Remember: trout and bass need bugs; bugs need weeds; and weeds need light.

Light can only penetrate so far. Weed growth can sustain bug life down to 15 feet. The exception is when fishing Chironomid (midge larvae) imitations, because they don't require weed growth.

Next, a stillwater angler needs mobility. On a small lake, the fisherman can get by with tennis shoes. On bigger water, a canoe, pram, kayak or float tube is a good choice.

After mobility, the fisherman has to reach the quarry. The troller or still-fisherman can lengthen leaders and add or subtract weight as necessary. The object is finding the feeders and finding them fast.

The fly-fisherman can get by with one or two lines. The most important is the slow-sinking clear intermediate fly line. Trout eat more than 90 percent of their food below the surface. A floating line is important and a type 3 sinking line can reach fish faster in deeper water.

It's all about finding active fish. Trout can be anywhere in the water column. For the best action, you have to identify where bugs and trout or bass are most active.

When fishing subsurface, that last two or three feet of line between leader and fly should always be fluorocarbon. That extra bit of stealth makes all the difference when it comes to bringing fish to the net.

Sometimes the best way to divine depth and isolate action is by sight. There's no better tool than a pair of polarized glasses to cut the glare. Shadows shift and clouds obscure the sun. For a moment, windows open in the blue-green water and the lake is opened like a book.

HATCHES

INSECT HATCHES	JAN	FEB	MAR	APR	MAY	JUN	JUL	AUG	SEP	OCT	NOV	DEC
1. *Hexagenia*					•	•	•					
2. *Callibaetis* Mayfly				•	•	•	•	•	•	•		
3. Longhorn Caddis					•	•	•					
4. Gray Drake							•	•	•			
5. Northern Case-Maker									•	•		
6. Midge	•	•	•	•	•	•	•	•	•	•	•	•
7. Dragonfly						•	•	•				
8. Damselfly						•	•					
9. Water Boatman									•	•	•	
10. Grasshopper							•	•	•			
11. Beetle							•	•	•			
12. Ant						•	•	•	•	•		

Important Foods (non-insect)	JAN	FEB	MAR	APR	MAY	JUN	JUL	AUG	SEP	OCT	NOV	DEC
13. Crayfish				•	•	•	•	•	•	•	•	
14. Snails				•	•	•	•	•	•	•	•	
15. Leeches	•	•	•	•	•	•	•	•				•
16. Sculpin	•	•	•	•	•	•	•	•	•	•	•	•
17. Scuds	•	•	•	•	•	•	•	•			•	•

INSECTS

1. *Hexagenia*

2. *Callibaetis* Mayfly

3. Longhorn Caddis or Black Dancer

4. Gray Drake

5. Northern Case-Maker

6. Midge

7. Dragonfly

8. Damselfly

9. Water Boatman

10. Grasshopper

11. Beetle

12. Ant

Important Foods (non-insect)

13. Crayfish

14. Snails

15. Leeches

16. Sculpin

OREGON STILLWATER SPORTFISH

Rainbow Trout

Cutthroat Trout

Brown Trout

Brook Trout

Bull Trout

Smallmouth Bass

Largemouth Bass

Channel Catfish

Black Crappie

Lake Trout *(mackinaw)*

Bluegill

Kokanee

Atlantic Salmon

FLY PATTERNS FOR TROUT

Comparadun (PMD)	Morrish Mouse	Dixie Devil Flyrod Popper	Callibaetis Emerger	AP Nymph (gray)	Callibaetis Nymph
Clouser Minnow	Renegade	Parachute Foam Hexagenia Mayfly	Hopper	Damsel Nymph	Dragonfly Nymph
Ice Cream Cone (Chironomid)	Prince Nymph	Hare's Ear	Pheasant Tail Nymph	Peacock Creeper	San Juan Worm
Water Boatman	Crystal Bugger	Thin Mint Woolly Bugger	Woolly Bugger (brown)	Carey Bugger (Olive)	Hale Bopp Bugger

FISHING TACKLE

Spoons / Spinners / Crankbaits

Acme Little Cleo Spoon	Dick Nite Spoon	Rooster Tail	Mepps Black Fury	Mack's Wedding Ring Pro	Rapala Countdown
Luhr Jensen Kwikfish K5	Matzuo SWTS-492	Lucky Craft Pointer	Fatfish	Luhr Jensen Speed Trap	AC Casitas 6-inch Swim Bait
Rock'N Runner Spinnerbait	BOOYAH Bi-You Buzz Spinnerbait	Strike King Bitsy Bug Jig	Lead Jig Head	Outlaw Pink Plastic Worm	Jackall Flick Shake Worm

Swim Baits / Spinner Baits / Jigs and Plastics

Baits / Floats / Weight / Trolling

Luhr Jensen Crippled Herring	*Berkley Gulp!* Salmon Eggs	Pautzke's Gold Label Balls O'Fire	A-Justa Bubble Casting Float	Bullet Sliding Sinker	Mack's Flash Lite Trolls

Jim Schollmeyer photographs

FISHING KNOTS

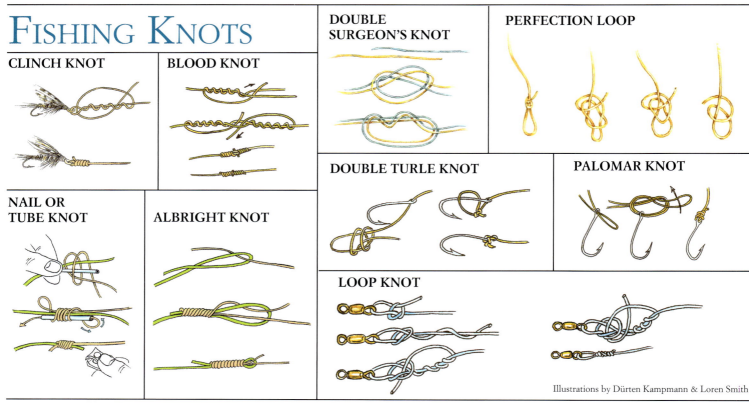

CLINCH KNOT

BLOOD KNOT

NAIL OR TUBE KNOT

ALBRIGHT KNOT

DOUBLE SURGEON'S KNOT

PERFECTION LOOP

DOUBLE TURLE KNOT

PALOMAR KNOT

LOOP KNOT

Illustrations by Dürten Kampmann & Loren Smith

FLY-FISHING TECHNIQUES

TWO-FLY NYMPH CHIRONOMID AND INDICATOR RIG

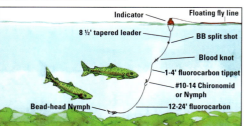

- Indicator
- Floating fly line
- 8 ½' tapered leader
- BB split shot
- Blood knot
- 1-4' fluorocarbon tippet
- #10-14 Chironomid or Nymph
- Bead-head Nymph
- 12-24' fluorocarbon

DRY-FLY DEAD-DRIFT TO RISING TROUT

- Dry fly
- Current
- 8' to 12' leader with tippet
- Floating weight-forward or double-taper fly line

WEIGHTED STREAMER RETRIEVE/ INTERMEDIATE LINE LEECH RETRIEVE

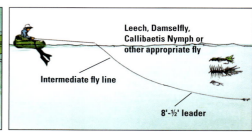

- Leech, Damselfly, Callibaetis Nymph or other appropriate fly
- Intermediate fly line
- 8'-½' leader

WIND DRIFTING/TROLLING

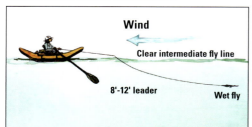

- Wind
- Clear intermediate fly line
- 8'-12' leader
- Wet fly

DRAGONFLY/DAMSELFLY NYMPH RETRIEVES

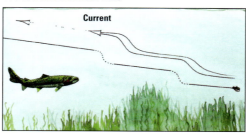

- Current

DRY FLY WITH DROPPER NYMPH/ CHIRONOMID

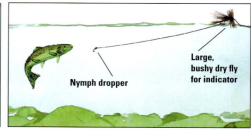

- Large, bushy dry fly for indicator
- Nymph dropper

COUNTDOWN METHOD FOR SINKING FLY LINE

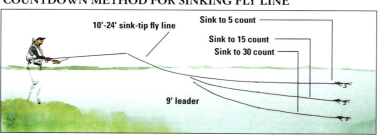

- 10'-24' sink-tip fly line
- Sink to 5 count
- Sink to 15 count
- Sink to 30 count
- 9' leader

Illustrations by Dave Hall

Trout/Kokanee Gear–Fishing Techniques

SPINNER AND WORM TROLL

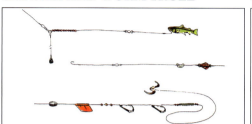

KOKANEE WEDDING RING SPINNER AND CORN TROLL

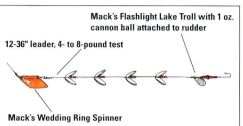

Mack's Flashlight Lake Troll with 1 oz. cannon ball attached to rudder

12-36" leader, 4- to 8-pound test

Mack's Wedding Ring Spinner

DOWNRIGGER LAKE TROUT TROLL

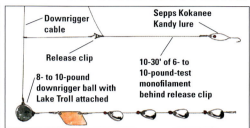

Downrigger cable

Sepps Kokanee Kandy lure

Release clip

8- to 10-pound downrigger ball with Lake Troll attached

10-30' of 6- to 10-pound-test monofilament behind release clip

SLIDING SINKER AND JAR BAIT

Power Bait, Gulp or Yum Dough bait

1 to 5 feet of 2- to 8-pound leader

#12 barrel swivel

3/8-ounce egg sinker

#12 to #16 Treble Hook

BOBBER AND BAIT

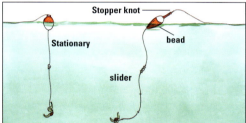

Stopper knot

Stationary

bead

slider

SPINNING–ROD FLY AND BUBBLE

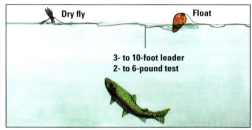

Dry fly

Float

3- to 10-foot leader
2- to 6-pound test

CASTING LURES: INJURED– MINNOW IMITATION; SPOON; SPINNER

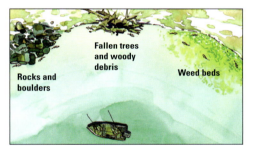

Fallen trees and woody debris

Rocks and boulders

Weed beds

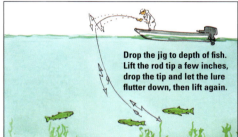

Drop the jig to depth of fish. Lift the rod tip a few inches, drop the tip and let the lure flutter down, then lift again.

KOKANEE/ TROUT JIGGING

Bass/Panfish Techniques

WACKY WORM RIG

CAROLINA RIG

12- to 48-inch
10- to 20-pound leader

1/4-1-ounce bullet weight

Barrel swivel

Plastic worm

Wide-gap bait hook

Mainline

Glass bead

SPINNER BAIT

CRAPPIE JIG

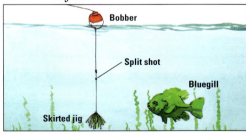

Bobber

Split shot

Bluegill

Skirted jig

DROPSHOT

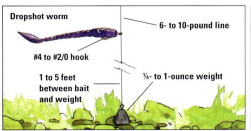

Dropshot worm

6- to 10-pound line

#4 to #2/0 hook

1 to 5 feet between bait and weight

¼- to 1-ounce weight

CRANKBAIT

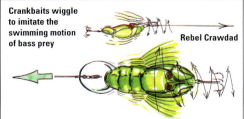

Crankbaits wiggle to imitate the swimming motion of bass prey

Rebel Crawdad

TOP–WATER PLUG/BUZZBAIT

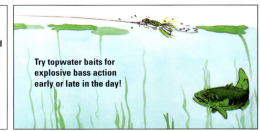

Try topwater baits for explosive bass action early or late in the day!

Illustrations by Dave Hall

Coffenbury Lake

In World War II, Coffenbury Lake bore much of the brunt of the Japanese attack on the U.S. mainland. When Fort Stevens was shelled, the enemy overshot the mark and put several salvos into this 50-acre freshwater pond.

Today, the water erupts with jumping rainbows. The Department of Fish and Wildlife allocates 13,000 legal and trophy rainbows for Coffenbury throughout the year. Weed growth and summer temps dampen trout fishing in June, July and August, but action picks up again in September and October. Trophy-size rainbows may be planted in September and will hold over through winter. Surplus steelhead from the nearby hatchery may be caught on anything from big spinners down to the most delicate of offerings.

A good place to bring the family, Coffenbury's banks have been developed to provide for still-fishermen. Wheelchair–accessible docks provide full access to the best fishing.

Jar baits are popular here because the stunted yellow perch seem to leave them alone. Fish with worms and you are more likely to end up battling minnows.

There are two ways to fish with bait, either suspended from a float, or on the bottom. To fish with a float, cut 24 inches of four-pound leader and connect it to the main line with a swivel. Tie a No. 8-10 hook to the end of the leader. The float will attach to the main line above the swivel. You may need to add lead weight above the swivel, depending on the type of bait you use. Worms or salmon eggs work well for trout when fished under a bobber.

Berkley Power Bait and similar "jar baits" are best used when fishing off the bottom. Slide a bullet sinker on your main line. Tie on a barrel swivel, then tie on a 36-inch leader and a small hook. Power Bait or a marshmallow in front of a piece of worm will keep your bait suspended off the bottom.

Many anglers fish from the bank, but car-toppers, float tubes and pontoon boats are a good fit. Trollers divide the lake into thirds, carving a pattern up and down the length of the lake.

Nearby options include Creep, Crawl and Crabapple lakes, as well as surf fishing in the ocean and angling for salmon and sturgeon at the mouth of the Columbia River.

With an aggressive trout-stocking program, Coffenbury Lake is capable of producing fast limits of fish, with a few fat rainbows for good measure. The bank is accessible for bank anglers and boaters.

VITAL STATISTICS

Surface Acres	56 acres
GPS coordinates	N 46 09.41' W 123 57.21'
Elevation	19 feet above sea level
Depth	22 feet

BEST TROUT/KOKANEE GEAR-FISHING TECHNIQUES

best	good	slow	Jan	Feb	Mar	Apr	May	Jun	Jul	Aug	Sep	Oct	Nov	Dec
Rainbow			1,6	1,6	1,6	1,5,6,7	1,5,6,7	1,5,6,7	1,5,6,7	1,5,6,7	1,5,6,7	1,5	1,6	1,6
Steelhead			4,6	4,6	4,6	4,6	1	1	1	1	1	1	4,6	4,6

1. Spinner and worm troll
2. Kokanee Wedding Ring spinner and corn troll
3. Downrigger lake trout troll
4. Casting Lures: Injured-minnow imitation; spoon; spinner
5. Sliding sinker and jar bait
6. Bobber and bait
7. Spinning-rod fly and bubble
8. Kokanee/trout jigging

BEST FLY-FISHING TECHNIQUES

best	good	slow	Jan	Feb	Mar	Apr	May	Jun	Jul	Aug	Sep	Oct	Nov	Dec
Rainbow			2	2	2	2	2,4	2,4	5,6	5,6	5,6	2	2	2
Steelhead			2	2	2	2	2	2	2	2	2	2	2	2

1. Two-fly Chironomid and indicator rig
2. Weighted streamer retrieve/intermediate line leech retrieve
3. Dragonfly/damselfly nymph retrieves
4. Dry-fly dead-drift to rising trout
5. Wind drifting/trolling
6. Dry-fly with dropper nymph/Chironomid
7. Countdown method for sinking fly line

SPECIES

RB	Rainbow trout
ST	Steelhead
YP	Yellow perch
BL	Bluegill
BB	Brown bullhead

AMENITIES

Resorts	No
Launches	One
Speed Limit	10mph
Campgrounds	Yes
Day–Use Area	Yes
Boat Rental	Seasonal

BEST FOR FISHING
March–May

OTHER FAMILY ACTIVITIES
• Fort Stevens State Park
• Wreck of the Peter Iredale – 1906
• Fort Clatsop National Memorial
• Clatsop County Historical Museum
• Fort Astoria
• Columbia River Maritime Museum
• Flavel House Museum
• Uppertown Firefighters Museum
• Scandinavian Midsummer Festival
• Astoria Column
• Cannon Beach
• Hiking
• Wildlife watching
• Swimming
• Camping
• Picnicking
• Soccer fields

LOCATION: Clatsop County

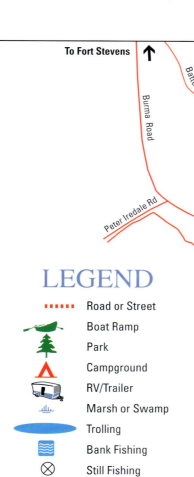

LEGEND

······	Road or Street
⛵	Boat Ramp
🌲	Park
⛺	Campground
🚐	RV/Trailer
⬩	Marsh or Swamp
⬭	Trolling
≋	Bank Fishing
⊗	Still Fishing

SERVICES

CAMPING/PARKS
• **Astoria/Warrenton/Seaside KOA,** Hammond, 97121, (800) 562-8506, (503) 861-2606, www.koa.com/campgrounds/astoria
• **Kampers West RV Park,** Warrenton, 97146, (503) 861-1814, www.kamperswest.com
• **Fort Stevens State Park,** Hammond, 97121, Reserve: (800) 452-5687, (503) 861-1671, www.oregonstateparks.org
• **Sunset Lake Resort & RV Park,** Warrenton, 97146, (503) 861-1760, www.sunsetlake.faithweb.com

ACCOMMODATIONS
• **Rose River Inn B & B,** Astoria, 97103, (888) 876-0028, (503) 325-7175, www.roseriverinn.com
• **Clementine's B & B,** Astoria, 97103, (503) 325 2005, www.clementines-bb.com
• **Grandview B & B,** Astoria, 97103, (503) 325-0000, (800) 488-3250, www.grandviewbedandbreakfast.com

TACKLE SHOPS/BOAT RENTALS
• **Englund Marine,** Astoria, 97103, (800) 452-6746 (Oregon only), (800) 228-7051 (nationwide), (503) 325-4341, www.englundmarine.com
• **Trucke's One-Stop,** Seaside, 97138, (503) 738-8863, www.shopseaside.com/trucke
• **Bud's RV Park & Tackle,** North Gearhart, 97138, (800) 730-6855, (503) 738-6855, www.budsrv.com
• **Coast Hardware,** Seaside, 97138, (503) 738-5491, www.coasthardware.com
• **Bakers General Store,** Seaside, 97138, (503) 755-2739, www.facebook.com

VISITOR INFORMATION
• **Astoria & Warrenton Chamber Of Commerce,** Astoria, 97103, (800) 875-6807, (503) 325-6311, www.oldoregon.com
• **Seaside Chamber of Commerce,** Seaside, 97138, (503) 738-6391, www.seasidechamber.com
• **Seaside Visitors Bureau,** Seaside, 97138, (800) 306-2326, (503) 738-3097, www.seasideor.com
• **Oregon Coast Visitors Association,** Newport, 97365, (888) OCVA-101 (628-2101), (541) 574-2679, www.visittheoregoncoast.com

NEAREST CITIES/TOWNS
Astoria, 97103; **Warrenton,** 97146; **Hammond,** 97121

Photo by Gary Lewis

Developed access at Coffenbury maximizes the fishing opportunity for families and anglers with limited mobility.

Cullaby Lake

Photo courtesy David Swendseid

This largest of the Clatsop Plain lakes was named for a Clatsop Indian known as Cullaby, and reputed to be the offspring of one of the members of the Lewis and Clark Expedition.

At two miles long, Cullaby Lake is fed by Cullaby Creek and several other small streams. Private timber companies own much of the land to the northeast and the lake retains a quiet demeanor because of the large tracts of forest. Skipanon River is the outlet, running six miles north to the Columbia.

Cullaby is stocked with rainbow trout in spring. Cutthroat trout are present in small numbers. Anglers find best success in April and May. Algae growth slows down trout fishing as the weather warms in late spring.

Fishing for bluegill, crappie, perch, bass and catfish picks up in May. The south end of the lake is reputed to have the best catfish.

For trout, hit Cullaby Lake early in the year. When temperatures climb, warmwater fishing improves. David Swendseid boated this great largemouth at Cullaby Lake.

BEST TROUT/KOKANEE GEAR-FISHING TECHNIQUES

best	good	slow	Jan	Feb	Mar	Apr	May	Jun	Jul	Aug	Sep	Oct	Nov	Dec
Rainbow			1,6	1,6	1,6	1,5,6,7	1,5,6,7	1,5,6,7	1,5,6,7	1,5,6,7	1,5,6,7	1,5	1,6	1,6
Cutthroat			1,6	1,6	1,6	1,5,6,7	1,5,6,7	1,5,6,7	1,5,6,7	1,5,6,7	1,5,6,7	1,5	1,6	1,6

1. Spinner and worm troll
2. Kokanee Wedding Ring spinner and corn troll
3. Downrigger lake trout troll
4. Casting Lures: Injured-minnow imitation; spoon; spinner
5. Sliding sinker and jar bait
6. Bobber and bait
7. Spinning-rod fly and bubble
8. Kokanee/trout jigging

BEST FLY-FISHING TECHNIQUES

best	good	slow	Jan	Feb	Mar	Apr	May	Jun	Jul	Aug	Sep	Oct	Nov	Dec
Rainbow			2	2	2	2	2,4	2,4	5,6	5,6	5,6	2	2	2
Cutthroat			2	2	2	2	2,4	2,4	5,6	5,6	5,6	2	2	2

1. Two-fly Chironomid and indicator rig
2. Weighted streamer retrieve/intermediate line leech retrieve
3. Dragonfly/damselfly nymph retrieves
4. Dry-fly dead-drift to rising trout
5. Wind drifting/trolling
6. Dry-fly with dropper nymph/Chironomid
7. Countdown method for sinking fly line

BEST BASS AND PANFISH TECHNIQUES

best	good	slow	Jan	Feb	Mar	Apr	May	Jun	Jul	Aug	Sep	Oct	Nov	Dec
Largemouth						1,7	1,7	4,6	4,6	4,6	1,7	1,7		
Crappie						3	3	3	3	3	3	3		
Bluegill						3	3	3	3	3	3	3		

1. Carolina rig
2. Spinner bait
3. Crappie jig
4. Dropshot
5. Crankbait
6. Top-water plug/buzzbait
7. Senko worm rig

BEST FOR FISHING

March–May (trout)

May–September (panfish)

OTHER FAMILY ACTIVITIES

- Fort Clatsop National Memorial
- Clatsop County Historical Museum
- Lindgren Cabin
- Cannon Beach
- Hiking
- Whale watching
- Wildlife watching
- Swimming
- Camping
- Picnicking

SPECIES

RB	Rainbow trout
CT	Cutthroat trout
BL	Bluegill
Cr	Crappie
YP	Yellow perch
LB	Largemouth bass
Cat	Catfish

Best bank access and good trout fishing can be found in the day–use areas on the west shore. Creek inlets offer the cold water that trout seek when temperatures climb in late spring and summer.

Clatsop County operates Cullaby Lake Park. Here, a nice boat ramp, dock, paved parking, restrooms, playground, horseshoe pits, shelters, picnic tables and beach are available for day use.

Nearby trout waters include Coffenbury Lake, Sunset Lake, Smith Lake and Lost Lake, all supported by ODFW stocking efforts.

LOCATION: Clatsop County

VITAL STATISTICS

Surface Acres	188 acres
GPS coordinates	N 46 05.716' W 123 54.751'
Elevation	8 feet
Depth	12 feet

AMENITIES

Resorts	No
Launches	One
Speed Limit	No
Campgrounds	Yes
Day–Use Area	Yes
Boat Rental	No

SERVICES

CAMPING/PARKS
- **Carnahan County Park,** Warrenton, 97146, (503) 325-9306, www.co.clatsop.or.us
- **Cullaby Lake County Park,** Warrenton, 97146, (503) 325-9306, www.co.clatsop.or.us
- **Astoria/Warrenton/Seaside KOA,** Hammond, 97121, (800) 562-8506, (503) 861-2606, www.koa.com/campgrounds/astoria
- **Kampers West RV Park,** Warrenton, 97146, (503) 861-1814, www.kamperswest.com
- **Fort Stevens State Park,** Hammond, 97121, Reserve: (800) 452-5687, (503) 861-1671, www.oregonstateparks.org
- **Sunset Lake Resort & RV Park,** Warrenton, 97146, (503) 861-1760, www.sunsetlake.faithweb.com
- **Bud's RV Park & Tackle,** North Gearhart, 97138, (800) 730-6855, (503) 738-6855, www.budsrv.com

ACCOMMODATIONS
- **Rose River Inn B&B, Astoria,** 97103, (888) 876-0028, (503) 325-7175, www.roseriverinn.com
- **Clementine's B&B, Astoria,** 97103, (503) 325 2005, www.clementines-bb.com
- **Grandview B&B, Astoria,** 97103, (503) 325-0000, (800) 488-3250, www.grandviewbedandbreakfast.com

TACKLE SHOPS/BOAT RENTALS
- **Englund Marine, Astoria,** 97103, (800) 452-6746 (Oregon only), (800) 228-7051 (nationwide), (503) 325-4341, www.englundmarine.com
- **Trucke's One-Stop, Seaside,** 97138, (503)-738-8863, www.shopseaside.com
- **Bud's RV Park & Tackle, North Gearhart,** 97138, (800) 730-6855, (503) 738-6855, www.budsrv.com
- **Coast Hardware, Seaside,** 97138, (503) 738-5491, www.coasthardware.com
- **Bakers General Store, Seaside,** 97138, (503) 755-2739, www.facebook.com

VISITOR INFORMATION
- **Seaside Chamber of Commerce, Seaside,** 97138, (503) 738-6391, www.seasidechamber.com
- **Seaside Visitors Bureau, Seaside,** 97138, (800) 306-2326, (503) 738-3097, www.seasideor.com
- **Astoria & Warrenton Chamber Of Commerce, Astoria,** 97103, (800) 875-6807, (503) 325-6311, www.oldoregon.com

NEAREST CITIES/TOWNS
Seaside, 97138; Warrenton, 97146; Hammond, 97121

To Warrenton

Astoria Country Club

● Carnahan

101

Cullaby Lake Ln

Carnahan County Park

Carnahan Park Ln

Taylor Lake

CLATSOP RIDGE

Hawkins Road

Boat Ramp

Cullaby Lake County Park

Cullaby Lake

West Lake

Anderson Road

Dellmoor Loop

Cullaby Creek

101

Oregon Coast Hwy

West Lake

To Seaside

0	.5	1 Mile

Devils Lake

This three-mile lake was named for an Indian legend about a monster that lived in the lake and occasionally dined on the natives. Like many of the lakes on the north coast, Devils Lake was formed when shifting sands dammed the river that drained the mountains. The D River, which empties the lake, is billed as The Shortest River in the World. Thompson Creek and Rock Creek are the major tributaries.

Lincoln City and the State of Oregon manage parks on the shores of this important recreational lake.

Once plagued by weeds, Devils Lake has been rid of that problem by the introduction of Chinese grass carp. The Devils Lake Water Improvement District is tasked with keeping the water clean. Their website (www.dlwid.

org) is a great reference for anglers.

Fin-clipped rainbows are the primary catch. 20,000 legals are stocked between early March and late April. Cutthroat trout, largemouth bass, bluegill, catfish and perch make their home in Devils Lake. Bass seem to prefer red and purple plastics. One of the best bass areas is in the northeast corner of the lake. Grass carp and coho salmon (silver-sided with intact adipose) must be released unharmed.

The best bank fishing can be found in the parks. Boats are available to rent. Trollers score with flashers early in the season. When the water warms, trout seek out the deeper holes and cold-water inlets.

Photo by Gary Lewis

At Lincoln City, Devils Lake is a good early-season bet for trout. March, April and May offer the best fishing.

SPECIES

RB	Rainbow trout
CT	Cutthroat trout
C	Coho
LB	Largemouth bass
CGC	Chinese grass carp
BL	Bluegill
BB	Brown bullhead catfish
YP	Yellow perch

BEST FOR FISHING

March–May

September–October

OTHER FAMILY ACTIVITIES

- Theaters
- Museums
- Oktoberfest
- Beachcombing
- Horseback riding
- Hiking
- Crabbing
- Birding
- Glass-blowing
- Tide-pooling
- Golfing
- Biking
- Deep-sea fishing
- Camping
- Picnicking
- Boating
- Whale watching

BEST TROUT/KOKANEE GEAR-FISHING TECHNIQUES

best	good	slow	Jan	Feb	Mar	Apr	May	Jun	Jul	Aug	Sep	Oct	Nov	Dec
Rainbow			5	5	1,4,8	1,4,8	1,4,8	1,4,5	5,8	5,8	5,8	5	5	5
Cutthroat			5	5	1,4,8	1,4,8	1,4,8	1,4,5	5,8	5,8	5,8	5	5	5

1. Spinner and worm troll
2. Kokanee Wedding Ring spinner and corn troll
3. Downrigger lake trout troll
4. Casting Lures: Injured-minnow imitation; spoon; spinner
5. Sliding sinker and jar bait
6. Bobber and bait
7. Spinning-rod fly and bubble
8. Kokanee/trout jigging

BEST FLY-FISHING TECHNIQUES

best	good	slow	Jan	Feb	Mar	Apr	May	Jun	Jul	Aug	Sep	Oct	Nov	Dec
Rainbow			2,7	2,7	2,7	1,2,5	1,2,5	1,2,5	1,2,5	1,2,5	2,7	2,7	2,7	2,7
Cutthroat														

1. Two-fly Chironomid and indicator rig
2. Weighted streamer retrieve/intermediate line leech retrieve
3. Dragonfly/damselfly nymph retrieves
4. Dry-fly dead-drift to rising trout
5. Wind drifting/trolling
6. Dry-fly with dropper nymph/Chironomid
7. Countdown method for sinking fly line

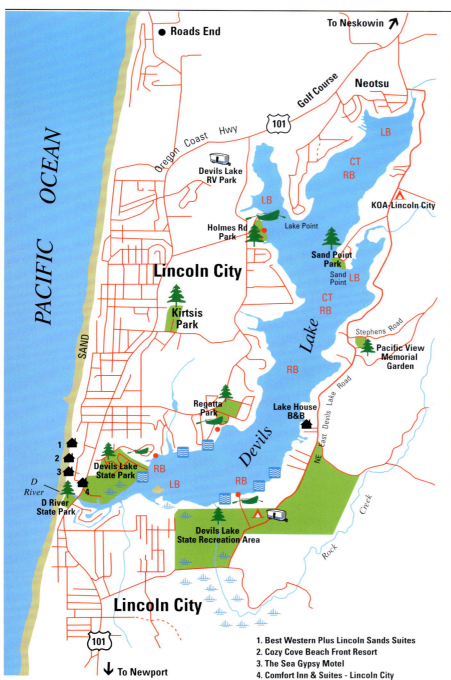

To Neskowin ↗

Roads End

Golf Course

Neotsu

101

Oregon Coast Hwy

Devils Lake RV Park

LB

CT
RB

LB

Holmes Rd Park

Lake Point

Lincoln City

Sand Point Park

Sand Point
LB

CT
RB

Kirtsis Park

Stephens Road

Pacific View Memorial Garden

RB

Regatta Park

Lake House B&B

Devils

Lake

NE East Devils Lake Road

Devils Lake State Park

1
2
3
D River
4

RB

LB

RB

D River State Park

Devils Lake State Recreation Area

Creek

Rock

Lincoln City

101

↓ **To Newport**

1. Best Western Plus Lincoln Sands Suites
2. Cozy Cove Beach Front Resort
3. The Sea Gypsy Motel
4. Comfort Inn & Suites - Lincoln City

SERVICES

CAMPING/PARKS
- **KOA-Lincoln City**, Otis, 97368, Reserve: (800) 562-3316, (541) 994-2961, www.koa.com
- **Devils Lake RV Park**, Lincoln City, 97367, (800) 460-0616, (541) 994-3400, www.devilslakervpark.com
- **Devils Lake State Recreation Area**, Otis, 97368, Info: (800) 551-6949, Reserve: (800) 452-5687, Park: (541) 994-2002, www.oregonstateparks.org
- **Logan Road RV Park**, Lincoln City, 97367, (877) 564-2678, (541) 994-4261, www.loganroadrvpark.com
- **Premier RV Resorts**, Lincoln City, 97367, (877) 871-0663, (541) 996-2778, www.premierrvresorts.com

COMMODATIONS
- **Salmonberry Inn & Beach House**, Lincoln City, 97367, (541) 921-0404, www.salmonberryinnandbeachhouse.com
- **Baywood Shores B&B**, Lincoln City, 97367, (800) 327-0486, (541) 996-6700, www.baywoodshores.com
- **Brey House B&B**, Lincoln City, 97367, (541) 994-7123, (877) 994-7123, www.breyhouse.com

TACKLE SHOPS/BOAT RENTALS
- **Blue Heron Landing Rentals**, Lincoln City, 97367, (541) 994-4708, www.blueheronlanding.net
- **Knight's Tackle Box**, Otis, 97368, (541) 994-8137
- **Siletz Moorage**, Lincoln City, 97367, (541) 996-3671, www.siletzmoorage.com

VISITOR INFORMATION
- **Lincoln City Chamber of Commerce**, Lincoln City, 97367, (541) 994-3070, www.lcchamber.com

NEAREST CITIES/TOWNS
Lincoln City, 97367; Otis, 97368

LOCATION: Lincoln County

N
W E
S

LEGEND

⬡	US Highway
	Road or Street
	Drift Boat Launch
🌲	Park
⛺	Campground
🚐	RV/Trailer
	Marsh or Swamp
	Bank Fishing

0   .5   1 Mile

AMENITIES

Resorts	Yes
Launches	5
Speed Limit	No
Campgrounds	Yes
Day–Use Area	Yes
Boat Rental	Yes

VITAL STATISTICS

Surface Acres	678
GPS coordinates	N 44 58.02' W 124 00.51'
Elevation	20 feet
Depth	21 feet

BEST BASS AND PANFISH TECHNIQUES

best	good	slow	Jan	Feb	Mar	Apr	May	Jun	Jul	Aug	Sep	Oct	Nov	Dec
Largemouth						1,4	1,4,7	1,4,7	1,6,7	1,6,7	2,6,7	2,5,7		
Bluegill							3	3	3	3	3	3		

1. Carolina rig
2. Spinner bait
3. Crappie jig
4. Dropshot
5. Crankbait
6. Top-water plug/buzzbait
7. Senko worm rig

Siltcoos Lake

Named for a local Indian chief, Siltcoos Lake is one of the most important freshwater fisheries on the coast. The lake was formed by sand dunes that dammed Siltcoos River, creating a large, shallow stillwater that drains a small basin in the coastal mountains.

The lake is fed by Woahink, Maple, Fiddle, and smaller creeks. Its outlet is Siltcoos River, winding its way to the sea. The 2 ½–mile river has been dammed, since 1963, to regulate lake levels and prevent saltwater intrusions.

Siltcoos has nice shallows and good insect life that grows wild cutthroats (to 20 inches and beyond) and big holdover rainbows (to seven pounds or more). Hatchery legal rainbows are stocked in spring. For trout, fish near the mouths of tributaries all season and fish the Kiechle Arm and north of Reed and Booth islands. The best fishing for rainbows is April and May and again in October and November. Sea-run cutthroat and steelhead can be part of the incidental catch in Siltcoos. Take care to release wild sea-runs unharmed.

Siltcoos' coho salmon fishery is a success story. The season opens October 1. Check current regulations before fishing.

In addition to excellent trout and salmon fisheries, warmwater fishing is some of the best on the coast. Bass fishing picks up as the water begins to warm in late winter, but the best fishing is from April through September. Bass-, bluegill- and perch-patterned crankbaits are a good bet, or try an Outlaw plastic worm in purple or blue.

Crappie start to bite in March and bluegill, yellow perch and catfish keep things interesting.

For something a little different, try Siltcoos River for trout or bass. Nearby lakes are also stocked with trout.

Several resorts, campgrounds and nearby coastal attractions make Siltcoos a great destination for fishermen and their families. The lake is located six miles south of Florence, along Highway 101.

Close to Florence, the beach, sand dunes and good camping, Siltcoos Lake has something for everybody in the family. Cutthroat trout, rainbows, salmon, steelhead, bass, crappie and other warmwater species make this lake an interesting fishery.

LOCATION: Lane & Douglas Counties

BEST BASS AND PANFISH TECHNIQUES

best	good	slow	Jan	Feb	Mar	Apr	May	Jun	Jul	Aug	Sep	Oct	Nov	Dec
Largemouth				1,3	1,3	1,3,4	1,2,7	2,5,7	5,7	2,6	2,6	1,4,7		
Crappie					3	3	3	3	3	3	3	3		

1. Carolina rig
2. Spinner bait
3. Crappie jig
4. Dropshot
5. Crankbait
6. Top-water plug/buzzbait
7. Senko worm rig

BEST TROUT/KOKANEE GEAR-FISHING TECHNIQUES

best	good	slow	Jan	Feb	Mar	Apr	May	Jun	Jul	Aug	Sep	Oct	Nov	Dec
Rainbow			1,5	1,5	1,5	1,4,5	1,4,5	5	5	5	1,4	1,4	1,5	1,5
Cutthroat			1,5	1,5	1,5	1,4,5	1,4,5	5	5	5	1,4	1,4	1,5	1,5
Coho												4	4	4

1. Spinner and worm troll
2. Kokanee Wedding Ring spinner and corn troll
3. Downrigger lake trout troll
4. Casting Lures: Injured-minnow imitation; spoon; spinner
5. Sliding sinker and jar bait
6. Bobber and bait
7. Spinning-rod fly and bubble
8. Kokanee/trout jigging

BEST FLY-FISHING TECHNIQUES

best	good	slow	Jan	Feb	Mar	Apr	May	Jun	Jul	Aug	Sep	Oct	Nov	Dec
Rainbow			2,5	2,5	2,5	2,3,5	2,3,5	2,3,5	2,7	2,7	2,5	2,5	2,5	2,5
Cutthroat			2,5	2,5	2,5	2,3,5	2,3,5	2,3,5	2,7	2,7	2,5	2,5	2,5	2,5
Bluegill					1,6	1,6	1,6	1,6	1,6	1,6	1,6	1,6		
Largemouth				2	2	2	2	2	2	2	2	2		
Crappie					2	2	2	2	2	2	2	2		

1. Two-fly Chironomid and indicator rig
2. Weighted streamer retrieve/intermediate line leech retrieve
3. Dragonfly/damselfly nymph retrieves
4. Dry-fly dead-drift to rising trout
5. Wind drifting/trolling
6. Dry-fly with dropper nymph/Chironomid
7. Countdown method for sinking fly line

SPECIES

CT	Cutthroat trout
RB	Rainbow trout
ST	Steelhead
C	Coho
Ch	Chinook
LB	Largemouth bass
Cr	Crappie
BL	Bluegill
YP	Yellow perch
Cat	Catfish

AMENITIES

Resorts	Yes
Launches	8
Speed Limit	No
Campgrounds	Yes
Day–Use Area	Yes
Boat Rental	Yes

LEGEND

 US Highway

Road or Street

 Hiking Trail

 Boat Ramp

 Park

Campground

 RV/Trailer

Trolling

Marsh or Swamp

0   .5   1 Mile

VITAL STATISTICS

Surface Acres	3164
GPS coordinates	N 43 53.035' W 124 06.856'
Elevation	8 feet
Depth	22 feet

OREGON DUNES
RECREATION AREA

SERVICES

CAMPING & PARKS
- **Driftwood II Campground,** Siuslaw National Forest, Reservations: (877) 444-6777, www.forestcamping.com
- **Tyee Campground,** Westlake, 97493, (541) 902-1369, www.reserveamerica.com
- **Nightingale's Fishing Camp,** Westlake, 97493, (541) 997-2892
- **Ada County Park,** Westlake, 97493, www.co.lane.or.us
- **Ada Fishing Resort,** Westlake, 97493, (541) 997-2342, www.adaresort.com
- **Lake's Edge RV Park & Marina,** Westlake, 97493, (541) 997-6056, www.lakesedgerv.com
- **Darlings Marina & RV Resort,** Florence, 97439, (541) 997-2841, www.darlingsresortrv.com
- **Siltcoos Lake Resort,** Westlake, 97493, (541) 999-6941, www.siltcooslakeresort.com
- **Siuslaw National Forest,** Tidewater, 97390, (541) 750-7000, Reservations: (877) 444-6777, www.fs.usda.gov
- **Lane County Parks,** Eugene, 97408, (541) 682-2000, www.lanecounty.org

ACCOMMODATIONS
- **Westlake Resort,** Westlake, 97493, (541) 997-3722, www.westlakeresort.com
- **Blue Heron Inn,** Florence, 97439, (541) 997-4091, (800) 997-7780, www.blueheroninnflorence.com
- **Woahink Lake Suites,** Florence, 97439, Reservations: 800-WOAHINK (962-4465), (541) 997-6516, www.woahinklakesuites.com

TACKLE SHOPS/BOAT RENTALS
- **Deep Down Baits,** Florence, 97439, (541) 991-7712
- **Darlings Marina & RV Resort** (Boat Rentals), Florence, 97439, (541) 997-2841, www.darlingsresortrv.com

VISITOR INFORMATION
- **Oregon Dunes Recreation Area,** Reedsport, 97467, (541) 271-6000, www.fs.usda.gov
- **Florence Area Chamber of Commerce & Visitor Center,** Florence, 97439, (541) 997-3128, www.florencechamber.com

NEAREST CITIES/TOWNS
Westlake, 97493; Florence, 97439

BEST FOR FISHING
April–October

OTHER FAMILY ACTIVITIES
- 4th of July Celebration
- Florence Rods 'n Rhodies
- Blues & Brews
- Rhododendron Festival
- Winter Folk Festival
- Ocean beaches
- Go-carts
- Honeyman State Park
- Sand dunes
- Hiking
- Biking
- Hunting
- Boating
- Picnicking
- Birding

Applegate Reservoir

Photo by Gary Lewis

Applegate Reservoir, near Medford, is stocked with an annual supply of 120,000 legal rainbows and 50,000 fingerling chinook. Good boat ramps, wheelchair facilities and plenty of camping, make it a great destination from the April trout opener through October.

Twenty three miles from Medford, at the base of the Siskiyou Mountains, Applegate Reservoir is a many-faceted jewel in Oregon's southwest corner. A forest of firs and pine trees surrounds the lake and the county road follows along the north bank. Hiking trails trace 18 miles of shoreline.

Construction of the dam was completed in 1980, creating a 988-acre flood-protection reservoir. The 4.6-mile reservoir is used to assure year-round flow in Applegate River.

Camping and recreation facilities are better than primitive, but have not lost their rustic character. There is a 10-mph speed limit to preserve peace on the water.

Applegate Reservoir's low elevation and warm temperatures contribute to a long growing season. Catchable rainbows and chinook salmon are stocked on a regular basis. Warmwater species are also available.

Applegate Reservoir is stocked with an annual supply of 120,000 legal rainbows and 50,000 fingerling chinook. This lake varies from a pool of 350 surface acres to almost 1000 acres, with a maximum depth of 225 feet. Good boat ramps, wheelchair facilities and plenty

LOCATION: Jackson County

BEST FLY-FISHING TECHNIQUES

best	good	slow	Jan	Feb	Mar	Apr	May	Jun	Jul	Aug	Sep	Oct	Nov	Dec
Rainbow						2,5	2,5	2,5	2,5,7	2,5,7	2,5	2,5		
Kokanee						5	5	5	5	5	5	5		

1. Two-fly Chironomid and indicator rig
2. Weighted streamer retrieve/intermediate line leech retrieve
3. Dragonfly/damselfly nymph retrieves
4. Dry-fly dead-drift to rising trout
5. Wind drifting/trolling
6. Dry-fly with dropper nymph/Chironomid
7. Countdown method for sinking fly line

BEST TROUT/KOKANEE GEAR-FISHING TECHNIQUES

best	good	slow	Jan	Feb	Mar	Apr	May	Jun	Jul	Aug	Sep	Oct	Nov	Dec
Rainbow						1,5,8	1,5,8	1,4,5	1,4,5	1,5	1,5	1,5,7		
Kokanee						8	8	2,8	2,8	2,8	2,8			

1. Spinner and worm troll
2. Kokanee Wedding Ring spinner and corn troll
3. Downrigger lake trout troll
4. Casting Lures: Injured-minnow imitation; spoon; spinner
5. Sliding sinker and jar bait
6. Bobber and bait
7. Spinning-rod fly and bubble
8. Kokanee/trout jigging

BEST BASS AND PANFISH TECHNIQUES

best	good	slow	Jan	Feb	Mar	Apr	May	Jun	Jul	Aug	Sep	Oct	Nov	Dec
Largemouth						1,7	1,4,7	1,5,7	1,5,6,7	1,2,5,6	2,5,6	2		
Smallmouth						3,4	5,7	5,7	5,7	5,7	2,3,4	3,4		
Crappie						3	3	3	3	3	3	3		
Bluegill						3	3	3	3	3	3	3		

1. Carolina rig
2. Spinner bait
3. Crappie jig
4. Dropshot
5. Crankbait
6. Top-water plug/buzzbait
7. Senko worm rig

AMENITIES

Resorts	Hart-Tish Store
Launches	3
Speed Limit	10mph
Campgrounds	5 (3 are drive-in)
Day–Use Area	Yes
Boat Rental	No

BEST FOR FISHING

April–October

OTHER FAMILY ACTIVITIES

• Sasquatch Trap, www.mdvaden.com/collings_mountain.shtml

• Hiking, 18 miles around the lake

• Boating

• Swimming

• Picnicking

• McKee Historic Covered Bridge, McKee

• Rogue Creamery, Central Point, www.roguecreamery.com

• Lillie Belle Farms Handmade Chocolates, Central Point, www.lilliebellefarms.com

VITAL STATISTICS

Surface Acres	988
GPS coordinates	N 123 06 42' W 42 03 18'
Elevation	1987 feet
Depth	225 feet

of camping, make it a great destination throughout the season.

The character of the lake lends itself to trolling for kokanee in the deep water near the dam and in the Squaw Creek arm. Best bank fishing is in the Middle Fork/Elliott Creek arm. Submerged standing timber provides good cover for largemouth bass. Smallmouth bass are found near rip-rapped banks and at transitions to deeper water. Crappie are targeted around submerged standing timber and in shallows near the inlets. Fly-anglers do well in Carberry Creek and Middle Fork/Elliott Creek arms and at the mouths of other tributaries.

In low water, French Gulch boat ramp is the best bet. There are swimming beaches at Hart-Tish campground and Seattle Bar Picnic Area. For seclusion, head to Harr Point and Tipsu-Tyee campgrounds by hiking trail or boat. RV camping is available at Carberry, Watkins, Hart-Tish and French Gulch.

SPECIES

RB	Rainbow trout
K	Kokanee
Ch	Chinook
LB	Largemouth bass
SB	Smallmouth bass
Cr	Crappie

LEGEND

Forest Road	
Road or Street	
Hiking Trail	
Boat Ramp	
Park	
Campground	
RV/Trailer	
Bank Fishing	

0   .5   1 Mile

SERVICES

CAMPING & PARKS
- **Rogue River-Siskiyou National Forest**, Medford, 97504, (541) 618-2200, www.fs.usda.gov
- **Applegate/Star Ranger District**, Medford, 97501, (541) 899-3800, www.ohranger.com
- **Jackson County Parks**, Central Point, 97502, (541) 774-8183, www.co.jackson.or.us
- **Applegate Lake Campgrounds**, www.applegatelake.com
- **Carberry Campground**, (541) 899-9220, www.applegatelake.com
- **Watkins Campground**, (541) 899-9220, www.applegatelake.com
- **French Gulch Campground**, Jacksonville, 97530, (541) 899-3800, publiclands.org
- **Harr Point Campground**, (541) 899-3800, publiclands.org
- **Hart-Tish Campground**, reservations: (877) 444-6777, www.applegatelake.com

ACCOMMODATIONS
- **White House B&B**, Medford, 97504, (541) 301-2086, www.thewhitehouse-bedandbreakfast.com
- **Bybee's Historic Inn**, Jacksonville, 97530, (541) 899-0106, (877) 292-3374, www.bybeeshistoricinn.com
- **Elan Guest Suites**, Jacksonville, (877) 789-1952, (541) 899-8000, www.elanguestsuites.com

TACKLE SHOPS/BOAT RENTALS
- **Hart-Tish General Store** (tackle & kayak rental), (541) 899-9220, www.applegatelake.com
- **Sportsman's Warehouse**, Medford, 97504, (541) 732-3700, www.sportsmanswarehouse.com
- **Black Bird Sporting Goods**, Medford, 97501, (541) 779-5431, www.blackbirdshoppingcenter.com
- **Bi-Mart**, Medford, 97501, (541) 779-8010, www.bimart.com
- **Carson's Guide Service**, Trail, 97541, (541) 261-3279, www.fishwithcarson.com
- **Carters Guide Service**, Medford, 97501, (541) 951-4700

VISITOR INFORMATION
- **Oregon Dunes Recreation Area**, Reedsport, 97467, (541) 271-6000, www.fs.usda.gov
- **Florence Area Chamber of Commerce & Visitor Center**, Florence, 97439, (541) 997-3128, www.florencechamber.com

NEAREST CITIES/TOWNS
Shady Cove, 97539; **Jacksonville**, 97530; **Medford**, 97504/97501

Diamond Lake

A jewel set in a glacier-scoured valley between Mt. Thielsen and Mt. Bailey, Diamond Lake was named for John Diamond, who discovered it in 1852. For fishermen who have sampled its nutrient-rich waters, it sparkles in memory. And a lot of anglers have plumbed her depths since the lake was originally stocked by pioneer pack train.

Two paved highways intersect at Diamond Lake, bringing anglers from Medford, Roseburg, Bend, Klamath Falls and beyond. It's a great place to bring the family. There has been a resort on Diamond Lake since the 1920s. Today, accommodations range from primitive lake-shore campsite to motel to vintage cabin to a four-bedroom family cabin.

Diamond Lake was poisoned, in late 2006, to rid the lake of the invasive tui chub. The lake was drawn down and then commercial fishing nets were used to haul out about a third of the chub. Then ODFW administered rotenone to kill the remaining fish. Diamond's historically productive water bounced back. Clarity is at more than 40 feet. Zooplankton and insect life are healthy and that means the environment is optimum for rainbows to put on weight.

Photo by Gary Lewis

Gary Lewis at Diamond Lake. Fly-fishermen should be prepared with Chironomids, Callibaetis, caddis and ant patterns. When no insect activity is evident, prospect on a slow-twitch troll with a two-nymph setup.

At Diamond Lake, some of the best fishing is after ice-off, which happens in May most years. Action slows with the temperature spike in August, but picks up again in September.

SERVICES

CAMPING/PARKS

- **Diamond Lake Resort,** Diamond Lake, (541) 793-3333, www.diamondlake.net
- **Thielsen View Campground,** (541) 498-2531, www.fs.usda.gov/umpqua
- **Diamond Lake Campground,** (541) 498-2531, www.fs.usda.gov/umpqua
- **Broken Arrow Campground,** (541) 498-2531, www.fs.usda.gov/umpqua
- **Poole Creek Campground,** (541) 498-2531, www.fs.usda.gov/umpqua
- **Diamond Lake RV Park,** Diamond Lake, 97731, (541) 793-3318, www.diamondlakervpark.com

TACKLE SHOPS/BOAT RENTALS

- **Sportsman's Warehouse,** Medford, 97504, (541) 732-3700, www.sportsmanswarehouse.com
- **Black Bird Sporting Goods,** Medford, 97501, (541) 779-5431, www.blackbirdshoppingcenter.com
- **Bi-Mart, Medford,** 97501, (541) 779-8010, www.bimart.com

VISITOR INFORMATION

- **Umpqua National Forest,** Roseburg, 97471, (541) 957-3200, www.fs.usda.gov/umpqua
- **US Forest Service's Diamond Lake Information and Visitors Center,** (541) 498-2531
- **Travel Medford Visitor Information Center,** Medford, 97501, (800) 469-6307, (541) 776-4021, www.travelmedford.org

NEAREST CITIES/TOWNS
Diamond Lake, 97731; Medford, 97504, 97501

VITAL STATISTICS

Surface Acres	3214
GPS coordinates	N 43 11.02' W 122 09.57'
Elevation	5183 feet
Depth	52 feet

AMENITIES

Resorts	Yes
Launches	5
Speed Limit	10mph
Campgrounds	3
Day–Use Area	Yes
Boat Rentals	Yes

SPECIES

RB	Rainbow trout

LOCATION: Douglas County

BEST FOR FISHING
May–July

September–October

OTHER FAMILY ACTIVITIES
- Mt. Thielsen
- Crater Lake National Park
- Cat Ski Mt. Bailey
- Rogue-Umpqua Scenic Byway
- Snowshoeing
- Hiking
- ATV riding
- Horseback riding
- Mountain-bike path
- Pizza parlor
- Boating
- Birding
- Camping
- Picnicking
- Hunting
- Snowmobiling

The first year after the lake was killed (2007) ODFW stocked 178,000 fish and the aggressive campaign continued in 2008 with 278,000 fingerlings, legals and brood trout. More fish have gone in the water here than any other lake in the state in the last decade.

Some of the best fishing is right after ice-off, which happens in May most years. Action slows down with the temperature spike in August, but picks up again in September.

The best bank fishing is on the north and northwest shore, but most anglers use watercraft. Bring a boat or rent one at the resort. A 10-mph speed limit is in effect. Morning and late evening are the best times to fish, but trout will bite all day long. Jar baits, flashers with small spoons, plugs and flies are most effective.

Insect production is huge here. Fly-fishermen should be prepared with Chironomids, Callibaetis, caddis and ant patterns. When no insect activity is evident, prospect on a slow-twitch-troll with a two-nymph setup.

Whichever method you employ, the secret is finding feeders. Chances are they will be near weed beds or suspended, letting bugs come to them. Experiment with different depths until you hit the first fish.

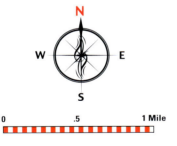

Diamond Lake

Thielsen View Campground

Diamond Lake Resort

North End Boat Ramp

South Shore Pizza

Campground

Campground

Boat Ramp

South Diamond Lake Campground

South Shore Boat Ramp

Broken Arrow Campground

Diamond Lake RV Park

Diamond Lake Bicycle Trail

UMPQUA NATIONAL FOREST

To Roseburg

Spruce Cr

Porcupine Cr

Camp Creek

Silent Creek

Teal Lake

Horse Lake

To Crater Lake

BEST TROUT/KOKANEE GEAR-FISHING TECHNIQUES

best	good	slow	Jan	Feb	Mar	Apr	May	Jun	Jul	Aug	Sep	Oct	Nov	Dec
Rainbow						1,4,8	1,4,5	1,5,6	1,5,6	1,5,6	1,5,6	1,5,6		

1. Spinner and worm troll
2. Kokanee Wedding Ring spinner and corn troll
3. Downrigger lake trout troll
4. Casting Lures: Injured-minnow imitation; spoon; spinner
5. Sliding sinker and jar bait
6. Bobber and bait
7. Spinning-rod fly and bubble
8. Kokanee/trout jigging

BEST FLY-FISHING TECHNIQUES

best	good	slow	Jan	Feb	Mar	Apr	May	Jun	Jul	Aug	Sep	Oct	Nov	Dec
Rainbow						2,5	2,3,5	2,5,6	2,5,6	1,2,5,7	1,2,5,7	2,5		

1. Two-fly Chironomid and indicator rig
2. Weighted streamer retrieve/intermediate line leech retrieve
3. Dragonfly/damselfly nymph retrieves
4. Dry-fly dead-drift to rising trout
5. Wind drifting/trolling
6. Dry-fly with dropper nymph/Chironomid
7. Countdown method for sinking fly line

LEGEND
- Forest Route
- Road or Street
- Hiking or Bicycle Trail
- Boat Ramp
- Park
- Campground
- RV/Trailer
- Marsh or Swamp
- Trolling
- Bank Fishing
- Still Fishing

Howard Prairie Lake

In 1958, engineers completed a rock-faced earthen dam on Grizzly Creek and water began to back up the old river-bed into grassy Howard Prairie and the tributary channels of Hoxie Creek and Willow Creek. Today, the impoundment is part of a network of storage reservoirs that involves the inter-basin transfer of water between Klamath and Rogue River watersheds. And it's one of the most important stillwater fisheries in Southern Oregon.

Rainbow trout are the most popular quarry, but largemouth and smallmouth bass are available. Fish grow fat in this food-rich water. Redear sunfish, bluegill and catfish keep it interesting when the bite slows for the glamour species.

The 2,070-acre lake is popular with boaters and bank-bound anglers alike. The best bank angling is at Red Rock near Willow Point campground, off the jetty near Resort at Grizzly Creek campground and other rocky faces. Wheelchair access from the jetty makes it easy for the physically-challenged.

Rainbows run 12 to 18 inches, but bigger fish are not uncommon. A two-year-old holdover can go well over 20 inches. PowerBait and Berkley Gulp! produce limits for still-fishers. The best bet is to use a four-foot leader to keep the bait out of weeds.

The old creek channel runs along the east shore. Trollers favor the north side of Buck Island and a triangle-route that runs from Red Rock to the store to the Hoxie Creek arm.

For bass, anglers target shoreside structure like willows in the Grizzly Creek arm and near Sugarpine campground. Other good spots (for bass and trout) include Doe and Fawn islands and the west bank, south of the resort.

When the water is cold, the south end of the lake seems to have the warmest temperatures, making the area near Sugarpine campground a better bet for bass. In warmer temperatures, trout fishing is best in deeper water.

Popular with boaters and bank anglers, Howard Prairie Reservoir is one of the most important stillwater fisheries in southern Oregon. Rainbows run 12 to 18 inches, but bigger fish are not uncommon. A two-year-old holdover can go well over 20 inches.

LOCATION: Jackson County

BEST TROUT/KOKANEE GEAR-FISHING TECHNIQUES

best	good	slow	Jan	Feb	Mar	Apr	May	Jun	Jul	Aug	Sep	Oct	Nov	Dec
Rainbow						1,4,6	1,4,5,6	1,4,5	1,5,8	1,5	5	5		

1. Spinner and worm troll
2. Kokanee Wedding Ring spinner and corn troll
3. Downrigger lake trout troll
4. Casting Lures: Injured-minnow imitation; spoon; spinner
5. Sliding sinker and jar bait
6. Bobber and bait
7. Spinning-rod fly and bubble
8. Kokanee/trout jigging

BEST FLY-FISHING TECHNIQUES

best	good	slow	Jan	Feb	Mar	Apr	May	Jun	Jul	Aug	Sep	Oct	Nov	Dec
Rainbow						1,2,5	1,2,3,5	1,2,3,4	1,7	1,7	1,4	1,2		

1. Two-fly Chironomid and indicator rig
2. Weighted streamer retrieve/intermediate line leech retrieve
3. Dragonfly/damselfly nymph retrieves
4. Dry-fly dead-drift to rising trout
5. Wind drifting/trolling
6. Dry-fly with dropper nymph/Chironomid
7. Countdown method for sinking fly line

BEST BASS AND PANFISH TECHNIQUES

best	good	slow	Jan	Feb	Mar	Apr	May	Jun	Jul	Aug	Sep	Oct	Nov	Dec
Largemouth						1,7	1,7	2,4,5	2,4,5	2,6,7	2,6,7	2,5		
Smallmouth						1,7	1,7	2,4,5	2,4,5	2,6,7	2,6,7	2,5		
Bluegill						3	3	3	3	3	3	3		

1. Carolina rig
2. Spinner bait
3. Crappie jig
4. Dropshot
5. Crankbait
6. Top-water plug/buzzbait
7. Senko worm rig

BEST FOR FISHING
May–October

OTHER FAMILY ACTIVITIES
- Boating
- Swimming
- Picnicking
- Hunting
- Hiking
- Horseback trails
- Four-wheeler trails
- Snowmobile trails

AMENITIES

Resorts	Yes
Launches	4
Speed Limit	No
Campgrounds	5 (public and private)
Day-Use Area	Yes
Boat Rental	Yes

SERVICES

CAMPING/PARKS

- **Klum Landing Campground,** (541) 774-8183, www.co.jackson.or.us
- **Sugar Pine Campground,** (541) 774-8183, www.co.jackson.or.us
- **Apserkaha Campground,** (541) 774-8183, www.co.jackson.or.us
- **Willow Point Campground,** (541) 774-8183, www.co.jackson.or.us
- **Grizzly Park Campground,** (541) 774-8183, www.co.jackson.or.us
- **Lily Glen Campground,** (541) 774-8183, www.co.jackson.or.us
- **Howard Prairie Resort Campground,** (541) 774-8183, www.co.jackson.or.us

ACCOMMODATIONS

- **Lithia Springs Resort,** Ashland, 97520, (800) 482-7128, (541) 482-7128, www.lithiaspringsresort.com
- **Green Springs Inn,** Ashland, 97520, (541) 890-6435, www.greenspringsinn.com
- **The Iris Inn, Ashland,** 97520, (541) 488-2286, (800) 460-7650, www.irisinnbb.com

TACKLE SHOPS/BOAT RENTALS

- **Sportsman's Warehouse,** Medford, 97504, (541) 732-3700, www.sportsmanswarehouse.com

- **Black Bird Sporting Goods,** Medford, 97501, (541) 779-5431, www.blackbirdshoppingcenter.com
- **Howard Prairie Resort Campground (boat rental),** (541) 774-8183, www.co.jackson.or.us,
- **Bi-Mart,** Ashland, 97520, (541) 482-8510, www.bimart.com
- **Carters Guide Service,** Medford, 97504, (541) 951-4700
- **Carson's Guide Service,** Trail, 97541, (541) 261-3279, www.fishwithcarson.com

VISITOR INFORMATION

- **Travel Medford Visitor Information Center,** Medford, 97501, (800) 469-6307, (541) 776-4021, www.travelmedford.org
- **Howard Prairie Lake Recreation Area,** (541) 774-8183, www.co.jackson.or.us.org
- **Jackson County Parks,** Central Point, 97502, (541) 774-8183
- **Rogue River-Siskiyou National Forest,** Medford, 97504, (541) 618-2200, www.fs.usda.gov

NEAREST CITIES/TOWNS

Ashland, 97520; Medford, 97504, 97501

SPECIES

RB	**Rainbow trout**
LB	**Largemouth bass**
SB	**Smallmouth bass**
RS	**Redear sunfish**
BL	**Bluegill**

VITAL STATISTICS

Surface Acres	2070
GPS coordinates	N 42 12.45' W 122 22.25'
Elevation	4526 feet above sea level
Depth	80 feet

LEGEND

⊶	Forest Route
▬▬▪▪▪	Road or Street
·······🚶	Hiking or Bicycle Trail
🛶	Boat Ramp
🌲	Park
⛺	Campground
🚐	RV/Trailer
〰	Marsh or Swamp
⬭	Trolling
〰	Bank Fishing
⊗	Still Fishing

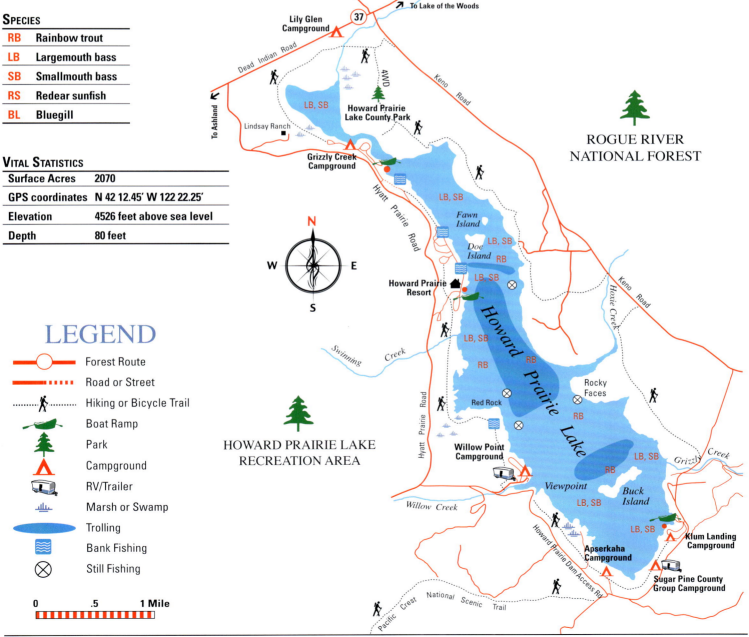

ROGUE RIVER NATIONAL FOREST

HOWARD PRAIRIE LAKE RECREATION AREA

0 .5 1 Mile

Hyatt Lake

Photo by Gary Lewis

Hyatt Lake has 950 surface acres and big rainbows. The shallow reservoir grows lots of insects. Trout and hatchery steelhead average 14 to 20 inches.

Jackson County's Hyatt Lake was once renowned for its rainbow trout fishery, but in recent years, largemouth-bass fishing has eclipsed angling for trophy rainbows. However, ODFW continues to stock trout and fishing can be very good early in the season.

In the shadow of Mt. McLoughlin this 957-acre irrigation reservoir is set in a flooded meadow in the mountains east of Ashland.

Most anglers bring a boat or rent one at the resort. Trout grow fast in this nutrient-rich water. Some of the biggest are caught by fly-fishermen. Streamer and Chironomids account for a lot of the fish.

For bank anglers, access is easy and good fishing can be found at Hyatt Lake Resort and at several other places around the lake. Roads follow the shoreline all the way around.

For still-fishing, use rainbow and chartreuse Power Bait or Gulp! in spring.

In fall, pink, red, and jar baits are productive. Use a sliding sinker and 40 inches of leader. Rig the bait on a No.16 treble hook. Cast, let bait sink to the bottom. Leave your bail open and let the fish take the bait.

Trollers also do well at Hyatt Lake and account for many of the fish that are taken every season. A few big fish fall to trollers, but the majority of their catch turns out to be smaller-sized trout. Summer brings the algae bloom and most anglers drop anchor and soak baits to avoid pulling in the salad.

For bass, fish the lake's perimeter. Throw plastic baits to standing timber

BEST FOR FISHING

May–October

OTHER FAMILY ACTIVITIES

- Camping
- Picnicking
- Birding
- Hiking
- Hunting
- Horseback trails
- Four-wheeler trails
- Snowmobile trails

AMENITIES

Resorts	1
Launches	1 - $5 fee
Speed Limit	10mph
Campgrounds	2
Day–Use Areas	Yes
Boat Rental	Yes

SPECIES

RB	Rainbow trout
LB	Largemouth bass
Bro	Brook trout

VITAL STATISTICS

Surface Acres	957
GPS coordinates	N 42 10 18' W 122 28 0'
Elevation	5016 feet above sea level
Depth	18 feet

SERVICES

CAMPING/PARKS
- **Campers Cove Resort & Restaurant,** Ashland, 97520, (541) 482-3331, www.hyattlake.com
- **Wildcat Campground,** Ashland, 97520, (541) 482-2031 (May-Oct) or (541) 618-2306, www.blm.gov/or
- **Horse Campground** (equestrian camp), Ashland, 97520, (541) 482-2031 (May-Oct) or (541) 618-2306, www.blm.gov/or
- **Hyatt Lake Recreation Complex,** Medford, 97501, (541) 618-2200, www.or.blm.gov/or

ACCOMMODATIONS
- **Lithia Springs Resort,** Ashland, 97520, (800) 482-7128, (541) 482-7128, www.lithiaspringsresort.com
- **Green Springs Inn,** Ashland, 97520, (541) 890-6435, www.greenspringsinn.com
- **The Iris Inn,** Ashland, 97520, (541) 488-2286, (800) 460-7650, www.irisinnbb.com

TACKLE SHOPS
- **Sportsman's Warehouse,** Medford, 97504, (541) 732-3700, www.sportsmanswarehouse.com

- **Black Bird Sporting Goods,** Medford, 97501, (541) 779-5431, www.blackbirdshoppingcenter.com
- **Bi-Mart,** Ashland, 97520, (541) 482-8510, www.bimart.com
- **Carson's Guide Service,** Trail, 97541, (541) 261-3279, www.fishwithcarson.com
- **Carters Guide Service,** Medford, 97501, (541) 951-4700

VISITOR INFORMATION
- **Travel Medford Visitor Information Center,** Medford, 97501, (800) 469-6307, (541) 776-4021, www.travelmedford.org
- **Howard Prairie Lake Recreation Area,** (541) 774-8183, www.co.jackson.or.us
- **Jackson County Parks,** Central Point, 97502, (541) 774-8183
- **Rogue River-Siskiyou National Forest,** Medford, 97504, (541) 618-2200, www.fs.usda.gov
- **Cascade-Siskiyou National Monument (BLM),** Medford, 97504, (541) 618-2200, www.blm.gov/or
- **Hyatt Lake Recreation Area,** Ashland, 97520, (541) 482-3331, www.blm.gov/or

NEAREST CITIES/TOWNS
Ashland, 97520; Medford, 97504, 97501

BEST TROUT/KOKANEE GEAR-FISHING TECHNIQUES

best	good	slow	Jan	Feb	Mar	Apr	May	Jun	Jul	Aug	Sep	Oct	Nov	Dec
Rainbow						1,4,6	1,4,5,6	1,4,5	1,5,8	1,5,6	5,6	5,6		

1. Spinner and worm troll
2. Kokanee Wedding Ring spinner and corn troll
3. Downrigger lake trout troll
4. Casting Lures: Injured-minnow imitation; spoon; spinner
5. Sliding sinker and jar bait
6. Bobber and bait
7. Spinning-rod fly and bubble
8. Kokanee/trout jigging

BEST FLY-FISHING TECHNIQUES

best	good	slow	Jan	Feb	Mar	Apr	May	Jun	Jul	Aug	Sep	Oct	Nov	Dec
Rainbow						1,2,5	1,2,3,5	1,2,3,4	1,7	1,7	1,4	1,2		

1. Two-fly Chironomid and indicator rig
2. Weighted streamer retrieve/intermediate line leech retrieve
3. Dragonfly/damselfly nymph retrieves
4. Dry-fly dead-drift to rising trout
5. Wind drifting/trolling
6. Dry-fly with dropper nymph/Chironomid
7. Countdown method for sinking fly line

BEST BASS AND PANFISH TECHNIQUES

best	good	slow	Jan	Feb	Mar	Apr	May	Jun	Jul	Aug	Sep	Oct	Nov	Dec
Largemouth						1,7	1,7	2,4,5	2,4,5	2,6,7	2,6,7	2,5		
Smallmouth						1,7	1,7	2,4,5	2,4,5	2,6,7	2,6,7	2,5		
Bluegill						3	3	3	3	3	3	3		

1. Carolina rig
2. Spinner bait
3. Crappie jig
4. Dropshot
5. Crankbait
6. Top-water plug/buzzbait
7. Senko worm rig

LOCATION: Jackson County

and flooded willows or crank spinnerbaits and minnow imitations. The cove by Willow campground is one good spot for largemouth. Another good spot is The Orchard, a big grove of dead, standing timber.

Wherever willows, brush, grass, tules or fallen timber create habitat and structure, bass can be found prowling the shallows. Throw watermelon-colored plastics, crankbaits and trout-pattern swimbaits to light them up.

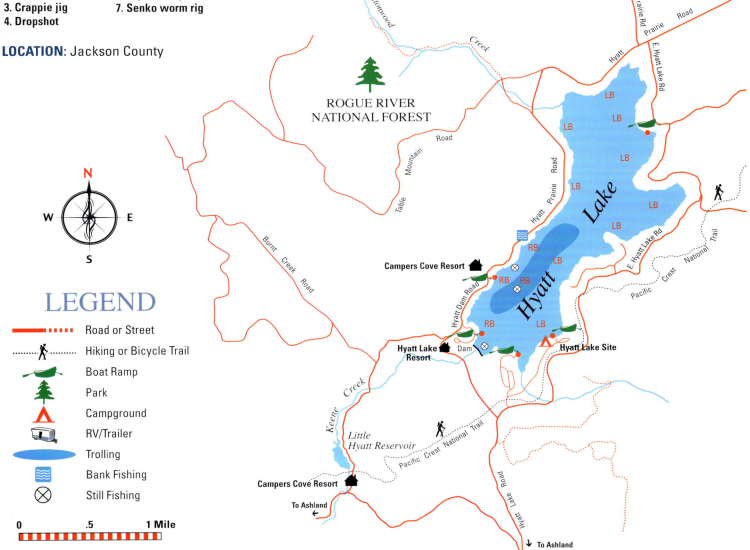

LEGEND

━━━ ┅┅┅	Road or Street
┈┈🚶┈┈	Hiking or Bicycle Trail
🛶	Boat Ramp
🌲	Park
⛺	Campground
🚐	RV/Trailer
⬭	Trolling
〰	Bank Fishing
⊗	Still Fishing

0   .5   1 Mile

Lake of the Woods

A large mountain stillwater in a forested setting, Klamath County's Lake of the Woods is a popular year-round destination. Dense stands of timber surround the 3 ½-mile lake.

Rainbow Creek on the south end of the lake and Blue Creek and Dry Creek on the north end are tributaries, but the majority of water comes from groundwater seepage. Seldom Creek is an outlet when the lake is at full pool, but evaporation counts for most of the water transfer.

The deepest water is found along the western shore, where the depth has been measured at 50 feet. Reportedly, there is a trench where the water reaches 90 feet, but few have found it. The average depth is 27 feet. There are weedbeds that foster insect growth, but rocky areas limit the spread of weeds. Kokanee are concentrated in the deepest water, across from Sunset Campground.

Each year Department of Fish and Wildlife supports LOTW with 11,000 to 12,000 rainbow and brown trout, stocked from the week before the April opener, through the end of August.

Lake of the Woods is famous for its brown trout fishing. Holdover browns grow large on the abundant food fish. Night-fishing for brown trout is legal and popular. Anglers connect with black-and-silver minnow imitations up to six inches long.

Some of the best trout fishing is found halfway between the resort and the western shore. Trollers score all up and down the west bank.

LOCATION: Klamath County

Catfish, crappie and perch were illegally planted here and are stunted because of overpopulation. Bass and brown trout get some of them, but anglers should keep all catfish, crappie and perch they catch to chip away at the numbers. Concentrate on fishing weedbeds and shallows at either end of the lake for warmwater fish.

Ice-fishing is good in January and February, when the ice is strong enough to support humans, tackle and bait. Contact the resort for a report on the ice pack.

Over 200 homes are situated on the banks of the lake. Lake of the Woods Resort is located on the eastern shore.

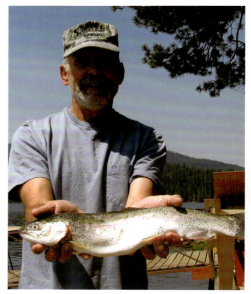

Bring your boat or rent one. Lake of the Woods is a great place to tie into a big rainbow or a brown trout.

BEST BASS AND PANFISH TECHNIQUES

best	good	slow	Jan	Feb	Mar	Apr	May	Jun	Jul	Aug	Sep	Oct	Nov	Dec
Smallmouth						1,4	1,4,7	1,4,7	5,6,7	5,6,7	2,5,6	2,7		
Crappie						3	3	3	3	3	3	3		
Bluegill						3	3	3	3	3	3	3		
Perch						3	3	3	3	3	3	3		

1. Carolina rig
2. Spinner bait
3. Crappie jig
4. Dropshot
5. Crankbait
6. Top-water plug/buzzbait
7. Senko worm rig

BEST TROUT/KOKANEE GEAR-FISHING TECHNIQUES

best	good	slow	Jan	Feb	Mar	Apr	May	Jun	Jul	Aug	Sep	Oct	Nov	Dec
Rainbow						1,5	1,4,5	1,5	1,5	5	1,4,5	1,4,5		
Brown						4,8	4,8	4	4	4	4,8	4,8		
Brook						1,5	1,4,5	1,5	1,5	5	1,4,5	1,4,5		

1. Spinner and worm troll
2. Kokanee Wedding Ring spinner and corn troll
3. Downrigger lake trout troll
4. Casting Lures: Injured-minnow imitation; spoon; spinner
5. Sliding sinker and jar bait
6. Bobber and bait
7. Spinning-rod fly and bubble
8. Kokanee/trout jigging

BEST FLY-FISHING TECHNIQUES

best	good	slow	Jan	Feb	Mar	Apr	May	Jun	Jul	Aug	Sep	Oct	Nov	Dec
Rainbow						2	2,3,5	1,2,3	1,2,3	1,2	1,2	2,7		
Brown						2	2,3,5	2	2	2	2	2		
Brook						2	2,3,5	1,2,3	1,2,3	1,2	1,2	2,7		
Perch						5	5	5	5	5	5	5		
Crappie						2	2	2	2	2	2	2		

1. Two-fly Chironomid and indicator rig
2. Weighted streamer retrieve/ intermediate line leech retrieve
3. Dragonfly/damselfly nymph retrieves
4. Dry-fly dead-drift to rising trout
5. Wind drifting/trolling
6. Dry-fly with dropper nymph/Chironomid
7. Countdown method for sinking fly line

SERVICES

CAMPING & PARKS
- **Sunset Campground,** Reserve: (877) 444-6777, www.recreation.gov
- **Lake of the Woods Resort,** Klamath Falls, 97601, (866) 201-4194, (541) 883-6714, www.lakeofthewoodsresort.com

ACCOMMODATIONS
- **White House B&B,** Medford, 97504, (541) 301-2086, www.thewhitehouse-bedandbreakfast.com
- **Klippness Hall B&B,** Klamath Falls, 97601, (541) 850-2586
- **Maverick Motel,** Klamath Falls, 97601, (800) 404-6690, (541) 882-6688, www.maverickmotel.com

TACKLE SHOPS/BOAT RENTALS
- **Lip Ripper Bait & Tackle Co,** Klamath Falls, 97601, (541) 884-8747, www.lipripperbaitandtackle.com
- **Sportsman's Warehouse,** Medford, 97504, (541) 732-3700, www.sportsmanswarehouse.com
- **Black Bird Sporting Goods,** Medford, 97501, (541) 779-5431, www.blackbirdshoppingcenter.com
- **Bi-Mart,** Medford, 97501, (541) 779-8010, www.bimart.com
- **Roe Outfitters,** Klamath Falls, 97603, (541) 884-3825, www.roeoutfitters.com

VISITOR INFORMATION
- **Medford/Jackson Chamber of Commerce,** Medford 97501, (541) 779-4847, www.medfordchamber.com
- **Ashland Chamber of Commerce,** Ashland, 97520, (541) 482-3486, www.ashlandchamber.com
- **Rogue River-Siskiyou National Forest,** Medford, 97504, (541) 618-2200, www.fs.usda.gov
- **Fremont-Winema National Forest,** Lakeview, 97630, (541) 947-2151, www.fs.fed.us
- **Travel Medford Visitor Information Center,** Medford, 97501, (800) 469-6307, (541) 776-4021, www.travelmedford.org
- **Ashland Ranger District,** (541) 552-2900
- **Klamath Ranger District,** (541) 885-3400

NEAREST CITIES/TOWNS
Ashland, 97520; Medford, 97504, 97501

AMENITIES

Resorts	Yes
Launches	One
Speed Limit	None
Campgrounds	5 (public and private)
Day-Use Area	Yes
Boat Rental	Yes

BEST FOR FISHING
May–October

OTHER FAMILY ACTIVITIES
- Camping
- Picnicking
- Boating
- Hiking
- Hunting
- Snowmobile trails
- **Rogue Creamery,** Central Point, www.roguecreamery.com
- **Lillie Belle Farms Handmade Chocolates,** Central Point, www.lilliebellefarms.com

SPECIES

RB	Rainbow trout
BT	Brown trout
Bro	Brook trout
K	Kokanee
LB	Largemouth bass
SB	Smallmouth bass
Cr	Crappie
BB	Brown bullhead catfish
YP	Yellow Perch

VITAL STATISTICS

Surface Acres	1146 acres
GPS coordinates	N 42 22.810' W 122 12.570'
Elevation	4949 feet above sea level
Depth	55-90 feet

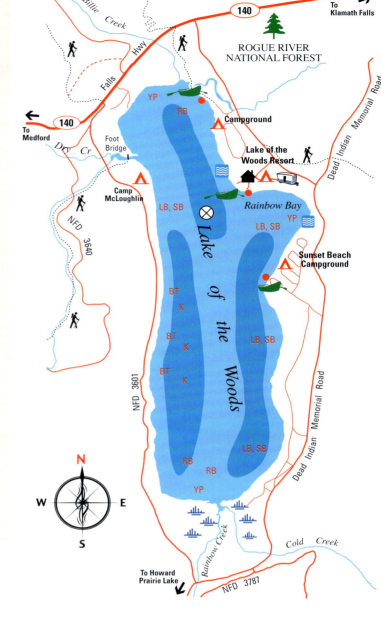

LEGEND

	State Route
	Forest Route
	Road or Street
	Hiking or Bicycle Trail
	Boat Ramp
	Park
	Campground
	RV/Trailer
	Marsh or Swamp
	Trolling
	Bank Fishing
	Still Fishing

Lost Creek Reservoir

Photo by Gary Lewis

3500-acre Lost Creek Reservoir has hatchery rainbows, cutthroats and browns. Try trolling a Wedding Ring spinner and a worm, a Rooster Tail, a Little Cleo or a Triple Teaze tipped with bait. This lake gets a good salmonfly hatch. When you see big bugs on the water, tempt trout and smallmouth bass with big dry flies.

Lost Creek Reservoir is a popular trout, bass and water-ski lake in the Rogue River watershed approximately 30 miles northeast of Medford. May and June are the most popular months for trout fishing. Bass fishing picks up as the water warms. In water-ski and jet-ski season, anglers find the most solitude in early mornings.

The lake is stocked with trout February through early June before Free Fishing Weekend. Trophy trout are stocked in September. Altogether, ODFW supports Lost Creek Reservoir with close to 85,000 trout.

The best bank fishing is near Stewart State Park boat ramp, Takelma boat ramp, near the out-take tower and the Highway 62 pullout near the dam.

Catfish Cove is another favorite spot.

Boats are available to rent from Lost Creek Marina. One of the best trolling areas is near the dam. Another good bet is to slow-troll the edge of the lake at mud lines and depth changes. Boat anglers also do well upstream from Highway 62 Bridge, whether trolling or wind-drifting with bait.

The river above Lost Creek Reservoir has rainbows, cutthroats and a few brown trout and brook trout. The mainstem and its tributaries open with the trout opener in April and close at the end of October. Anglers may keep five trout per day. There is no limit on the size or number of brook trout.

LOCATION: Jackson County

BEST TROUT/KOKANEE GEAR-FISHING TECHNIQUES

best good slow	Jan	Feb	Mar	Apr	May	Jun	Jul	Aug	Sep	Oct	Nov	Dec
Rainbow				1,5,8	1,5,8	1,4,5	1,4,5	1,5	1,5	1,5,7		
Cutthroat				4	4	4	4	4	4	4		
Brook				1,5,8	1,5,8	1,4,5	1,4,5	1,5	1,5	1,5,7		
Brown				4,8	4,8	4,8	4,8	4,8	4,8	4,8		

1. Spinner and worm troll
2. Kokanee Wedding Ring spinner and corn troll
3. Downrigger lake trout troll
4. Casting Lures: Injured-minnow imitation; spoon; spinner
5. Sliding sinker and jar bait
6. Bobber and bait
7. Spinning-rod fly and bubble
8. Kokanee/trout jigging

BEST FLY-FISHING TECHNIQUES

best good slow	Jan	Feb	Mar	Apr	May	Jun	Jul	Aug	Sep	Oct	Nov	Dec
Rainbow				2,5	2,5	2,5	2,5,7	2,5,7	2,5	2,5		
Cutthroat				2,6	2,6	2,6	2,6	2,6	2,6	2,6		
Brook				2,5	2,5	2,5	2,5,7	2,5,7	2,5	2,5		
Brown				2	2	2	2,7	2,7	2,7	2		

1. Two-fly Chironomid and indicator rig
2. Weighted streamer retrieve/intermediate line leech retrieve
3. Dragonfly/damselfly nymph retrieves
4. Dry-fly dead-drift to rising trout
5. Wind drifting/trolling
6. Dry-fly with dropper nymph/Chironomid
7. Countdown method for sinking fly line

BEST FOR FISHING

April–October

OTHER FAMILY ACTIVITIES

- Cole Rivers Hatchery
- Hiking
- Boating
- Swimming
- Picnicking
- Camping
- Hunting
- Casey State Park
- Joseph H. Stewart State Park
- Rafting (in Rogue River)

AMENITIES

Resorts	Yes
Launches	3
Speed Limit	No
Campgrounds	Yes
Day–Use Area	Yes
Boat Rental	Yes

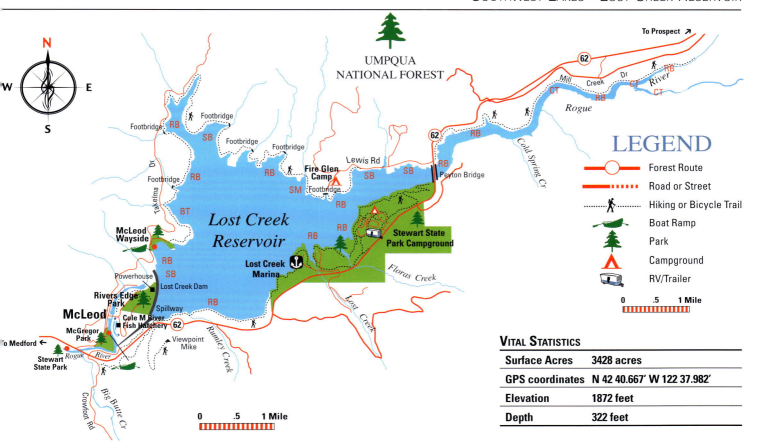

VITAL STATISTICS

Surface Acres	3428 acres
GPS coordinates	N 42 40.667' W 122 37.982'
Elevation	1872 feet
Depth	322 feet

SERVICES

CAMPING & PARKS

- **Casey State Recreation Site**, Info: (800) 551-6949, Park: (541) 560-3334, www.oregonstateparks.org
- **McGregor Park**, Trail, 97541, (BLM) (541) 618-2200, www.blm.gov/or
- **Lost Creek Marina & Restaurant**, Trail, 97541, (541) 560-3646, www.lostcreeklakemarina.wordpress.com
- **Joseph H. Stewart State Recreation Area**, Trail, 97541, Reserve: (800) 452-5687, Info: (800) 551-6949, Park: (541) 560-3334, www.oregonstateparks.org
- **Shady Trails RV Park**, Shady Cove, 97539, (541) 878-2206, www.gocampingamerica.com
- **Rogue River RV Park**, Shady Cove, 97539, Reserve: (800) 775-0367, Info: (541) 878-2404, www.rogueriverrv.com

ACCOMMODATIONS

- **White House B & B**, Medford, 97504, (541) 301-2086, www.thewhitehouse-bedandbreakfast.com

- **Maple Leaf Motel**, Shady Cove, 97539, (541) 878-2169, www.mapleleaf-motel.com

TACKLE SHOPS/BOAT RENTALS

- **The Fishin' Hole Fly Shop**, Shady Cove, 97539, (541) 878-4000
- **Carson's Guide Service**, Trail, 97541, (541) 261-3279, www.fishwithcarson.com
- **Lost Creek Marina & Boat Rentals**, Trail, 97541, (541) 560-3646, www.lost-creek-marina.com
- **Sportsman's Warehouse**, Medford, 97504, (541) 732-3700, www.sportsmanswarehouse.com
- **Black Bird Sporting Goods**, Medford, 97501, (541) 779-5431, www.blackbirdshoppingcenter.com
- **Bi-Mart**, Medford, 97501, (541) 779-8010, www.bimart.com

VISITOR INFORMATION

- **Travel Medford Visitor Information Center**, Medford, 97501, (800) 469-6307, (541) 776-4021, www.travelmedford.org

NEAREST CITIES/TOWNS

Ashland, 97520; Medford, 97504

BEST BASS AND PANFISH TECHNIQUES

best good slow	Jan	Feb	Mar	Apr	May	Jun	Jul	Aug	Sep	Oct	Nov	Dec
Largemouth				1,7	1,4,7	1,5,7	1,5,6,7	1,2,5,6	2,5,6	2		
Smallmouth				3,4	5,7	5,7	5,7	5,7	2,3,4	3,4		
Crappie				3	3	3	3	3	3	3		
Bluegill				3	3	3	3	3	3	3		

1. Carolina rig
2. Spinner bait
3. Crappie jig
4. Dropshot
5. Crankbait
6. Top-water plug/buzzbait
7. Senko worm rig

SPECIES

RB	Rainbow trout
CT	Cutthroat trout
Bro	Brook trout
BT	Brown trout
SB	Smallmouth bass
Cat	Catfish

Tenmile Lakes

Miles of shoreline with creek inlets, fingers, shallow bays, rocky structure, lily pads, submerged logs and hundreds of docks and houseboats, provide structure and habitat that make Tenmile Lake and North Tenmile two of the best bass lakes in the state.

Named for Tenmile Creek, which was supposed to be about 10 miles away from Winchester Bay, an early pioneer settlement, the Tenmile lakes are two natural lakes separated by a man-made channel.

The Tenmile watershed drains the west side of the Coast Range south of the Umpqua River. Black's, Wilkins, Murphy, Big creeks and several smaller streams feed North Tenmile. Tenmile tributaries include North Tenmile (via the channel) and Benson, Johnson, Adams and Shutter creeks. Tenmile Creek connects the lakes to the ocean.

There are few deep holes. The deepest spot is 22 feet down; the average depth is about 15 feet.

Jigs, plastics and crankbaits account for most of the bass. Work shoreline structure and experiment with different depths. Cast to pilings, docks and houseboats where bass wait to ambush their prey. The bass fishery is the main attraction on Tenmile and North Tenmile, but crappie, bluegill and catfish are abundant.

ODFW stocks the lakes with rainbow trout as well. April and May are the best months for trout fishing, but holdover rainbows can be caught throughout the season. Trout can grow large in this productive water.

The lake system is home to steelhead and salmon runs. The coho fishery is closed. Non-finclipped steelhead must be released.

There is a substantial, wheelchair-accessible public dock in Lakeside that is a great place for young and old to try their luck. There are no public campgrounds on either lake, but several private campgrounds and resorts serve the traveling angler. The nearest state campground is Spinreel on the banks of Tenmile Creek.

Tenmile Lake and its twin, North Tenmile, are famou for producing good catches of largemouth bass.

LOCATION: Coos County

VITAL STATISTICS

Surface Acres	1627 acres (Tenmile Lake)
GPS coordinates	N 43 34.374' W 124 10.435'
Elevation	9 feet
Depth	22 feet

AMENITIES

Resorts	Yes
Launches	5
Speed Limit	No
Campgrounds	Yes
Day–Use Area	Yes
Boat Rental	Yes

SPECIES

Cr	Crappie
BL	Bluegill
BB	Brown bullhead catfish
RB	Rainbow trout
CT	Cutthroat trout
C	Coho
ST	Steelhead
Stu	Sturgeon

BEST FLY-FISHING TECHNIQUES

best good slow	Jan	Feb	Mar	Apr	May	Jun	Jul	Aug	Sep	Oct	Nov	Dec
Rainbow	2,5	2,5	2,5	2,3,5	2,3,5	2,3,5	2,7	2,7	2,5	2,5	2,5	2,5
Cutthroat	2,5	2,5	2,5	2,3,5	2,3,5	2,3,5	2,7	2,7	2,5	2,5	2,5	2,5
Bluegill			1,6	1,6	1,6	1,6	1,6	1,6	1,6	1,6		
Largemouth		2	2	2	2	2	2	2	2	2		
Crappie		2	2	2	2	2	2	2	2			

1. Two-fly Chironomid and indicator rig
2. Weighted streamer retrieve/intermediate line leech retrieve
3. Dragonfly/damselfly nymph retrieves
4. Dry-fly dead-drift to rising trout

5. Wind drifting/trolling
6. Dry fly with dropper nymph/Chironomid
7. Countdown method for sinking fly line

BEST TROUT/KOKANEE GEAR-FISHING TECHNIQUES

best good slow	Jan	Feb	Mar	Apr	May	Jun	Jul	Aug	Sep	Oct	Nov	Dec
Rainbow	1,5	1,5	1,5	1,4,5	1,4,5	5	5	5	1,4	1,4	1,5	1,5
Cutthroat	1,5	1,5	1,5	1,4,5	1,4,5	5	5	5	1,4	1,4	1,5	1,5

1. Spinner and worm troll
2. Kokanee Wedding Ring spinner and corn troll
3. Downrigger lake trout troll
4. Casting Lures: Injured-minnow imitation; spoon; spinner

5. Sliding sinker and jar bait
6. Bobber and bait
7. Spinning-rod fly and bubble
8. Kokanee/trout jigging

BEST FOR FISHING

April–October

OTHER FAMILY ACTIVITIES

• Independence Day
• Cardboard Boat Races (August)
• Columbia Drag Boat Association Lakeside Races(August)
• Ocean beaches
• Sand dunes
• Hiking
• Biking
• Hunting
• Boating
• Swimming
• Picnicking
• Birding
• Clamming
• Crabbing

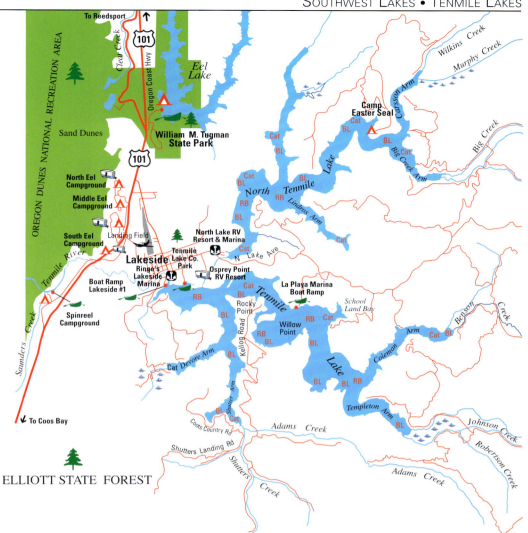

LEGEND

	Forest Route
	Road or Street
	Hiking or Bicycle Trail
	Boat Ramp
	Park
	Campground
	RV/Trailer
	Landing Strip or Airport
	Marsh or Swamp

0   .5   1 Mile

ELLIOTT STATE FOREST

BEST BASS AND PANFISH TECHNIQUES

best good slow	Jan	Feb	Mar	Apr	May	Jun	Jul	Aug	Sep	Oct	Nov	Dec
Largemouth		1,3	1,3	1,3,4	1,2,7	2,5,7	5,7	6,7	6,7	1,4,7		
Crappie			3	3	3	3	3	3	3	3		

1. Carolina rig
2. Spinner bait
3. Crappie jig
4. Dropshot
5. Crankbait
6. Top-water plug/buzzbait
7. Senko worm rig

SERVICES

CAMPING/PARKS

- **William M. Tugman State Park,** Reedsport, 97467,
  Reservations: (800) 452-5687, (541) 759-3604, www.oregonstateparks.org
- **North Lake Resort RV Park & Marina,** (541) 759-3515,
  www.northlakeresort.com
- **Tenmile Lake County Park,** Lakeside, 97449,
  reservations: (541) 396-7755, info: (541) 396-7759
- **Osprey Point RV Resort,** Lakeside, 97449, (541) 759-2801,
  www.ospreypoint.net
- **La Playa Marina,** Lakeside, 97449, (541) 759-4775
- **Spinreel Campground,** North Bend, 97459, (541) 271-6000,
  reserve: (877) 444-6777, www.fs.fed.us

ACCOMMODATIONS

- **Coos Bay Manor B&B,** Coos Bay, 97420, (800) 269-1224,
  www.coosbaymanor.com
- **The Old Tower House B&B,** Coos Bay, 97420, (541) 888-6058,
  www.oldtowerhouse.com
- **Edwin K B&B,** Florence, 97439, (541) 997-8360, 800-833-9465,
  www.edwink.com

- **Lakeshore Lodge,** Lakeside 97449, (541) 759-3161
  www.lakeshorelodgeor.com

TACKLE SHOPS/BOAT RENTALS

- **Spinreel Dune Buggy Rentals,** North Bend, 97459, (541) 759-3313,
  www.ridetheoregondunes.com
- **Stockade Market & Tackle,** Winchester Bay, 97467, (541) 271-3800
- **Englund Marine,** Coos Bay, 97420, (541) 888-6623,
  www.englundmarine.com
- **Basin Tackle Shop,** Charleston, 97420, (541) 888-3811

VISITOR INFORMATION

- **Lakeside Chamber of Commerce,** Lakeside, 97449, 541-759-3981,
  www.lakesideoregonchambers.com
- **Reedsport Chamber of Commerce,** Reedsport, 97467, (541) 271-3495,
  www.reedsportcc.org
- **Coos County Parks & Recreation,** reserve: (541) 396-7755,
  www.co.coos.or.us
- **Oregon Dunes National Recreation Area,**
  www.oregonsadventurecoast.com

NEAREST CITIES/TOWNS

Lakeside, 97449; Reedsport, 97467

Clear Lake
(McKenzie Watershed)

Linn County's Clear Lake is one of 11 in the state with the same name. Well-named, its clarity allows the angler to see 56 feet down. Born of volcanic fire, this 160-acre lake is the source of the McKenzie River. Dammed by lava flow, the lake is surrounded by evidence of recent volcanic activity and huge Douglas fir trees. In fact, an underwater forest is visible in the crystal-clear water.

Inflow comes from large springs on the north and east shore: Ikenick Creek and Big Spring. The lake is divided into two main pools by a narrow channel. The smaller section reaches a depth of 40 feet, while the biggest section has a depth down to 175 feet.

ODFW stocks rainbow and brook trout every spring and summer. Cutthroat trout are native. The temperature remains low enough for trout to thrive throughout summer. Bank anglers find success in both sections of the lake. The key is to cast beyond the shallows. All trout methods work here, but most anglers prefer to fish from a boat.

Trollers prefer the larger pool to the south along each bank as far down as Coldwater Cove. Fly-rodders may feel more at home tempting trout on the north end of the lake. Still-fishing pays off in both areas.

The lake is popular with ospreys as well as fishermen. When the water is clear, fish go deeper to stay out of danger. If the wind blows a riffle, trout elevate to feed closer to the surface.

Linn County owns the resort on the lake and operates a small restaurant and store. No motors are allowed. Rowboats are available to rent.

Photo by Gary Lewis

Lee Van Tassell admires a nice Clear Lake brook trout landed by son Matt.

LOCATION: Linn County

BEST FLY-FISHING TECHNIQUES

best	good	slow	Jan	Feb	Mar	Apr	May	Jun	Jul	Aug	Sep	Oct	Nov	Dec
Rainbow						1,2	1,2,3,4	1,2,3,4	1,2,3,4	1,2,3,4	1,2,3,4	1,2,3,4		
Cutthroat						1,2	1,2,3,4	1,2,3,4	1,2,3,4	1,2,3,4	1,2,3,4	1,2,3,4		
Brook						1,2	1,2,3,4	1,2,3,4	1,2,3,4	1,2,3,4	1,2,3,4	1,2,3,4		

1. Two-fly Chironomid and indicator rig
2. Weighted streamer retrieve/ intermediate line leech retrieve
3. Dragonfly/damselfly nymph retrieves
4. Dry-fly dead-drift to rising trout
5. Wind drifting/trolling
6. Dry-fly with dropper nymph/Chironomid
7. Countdown method for sinking fly line

BEST TROUT/KOKANEE GEAR-FISHING TECHNIQUES

best	good	slow	Jan	Feb	Mar	Apr	May	Jun	Jul	Aug	Sep	Oct	Nov	Dec
Rainbow						1,4,5,6	1,4,5,6	5,6,7	5,6,7	5,6,7	1,5,6	1,5,6		
Cutthroat						1,4,5,6	1,4,5,6	5,6,7	5,6,7	5,6,7	1,5,6	1,5,6		
Brook						1,4,5,6	1,4,5,6	5,6,7	5,6,7	5,6,7	1,5,6	1,5,6		

1. Spinner and worm troll
2. Kokanee Wedding Ring spinner and corn troll
3. Downrigger lake trout troll
4. Casting Lures: Injured-minnow imitation; spoon; spinner
5. Sliding sinker and jar bait
6. Bobber and bait
7. Spinning rod fly and bubble
8. Kokanee/trout jigging

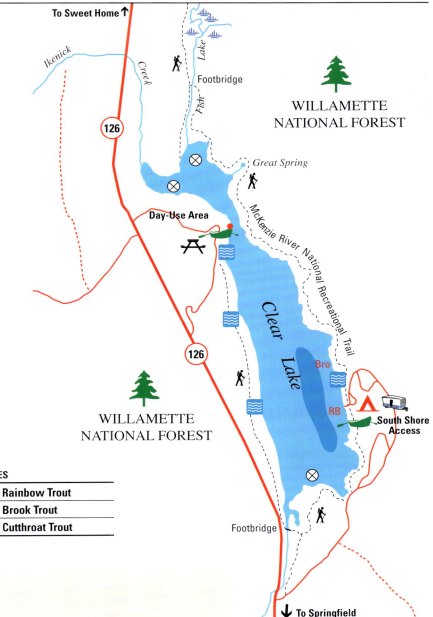

LEGEND

	State Route
	Road or Street
	Hiking or Bicycle Trail
	Boat Ramp
	Park
	Campground
	RV/Trailer
	Marsh or Swamp
	Bank Fishing
	Trolling
	Still Fishing

0   .5   1 Mile

Vital Statistics

Surface Acres	160 acres
GPS coordinates	N 44.36778 W 121.99306
Elevation	3012 feet above sea level
Depth	175 feet

Species

RB	Rainbow Trout
Bro	Brook Trout
CT	Cutthroat Trout

SERVICES

CAMPING/PARKS

- **Willamette National Forest,** www.fs.usda.gov/willamette
- **Coldwater Cove Campground & RV,** Reserve: (877) 444-6777, www.recreation.gov
- **McKenzie Bridge Campground,** Reserve: (877) 444-6777, www.recreation.gov
- **Cascadia State Park,** Park: (541) 367-6021, Info: (800) 551-6949
- **Belknap Hot Springs, Lodge & Gardens,** Belknap Springs, 97413, (541) 822-3512, www.belknaphotsprings.com

ACCOMMODATIONS

- **McKenzie River Inn,** Vida, 97488, (541) 822-6260, www.mckenzieriverinn.com
- **Eagle Rock Lodge,** Vida, 97488, Reservations: (888) 773-4333, (541) 822-3630, www.eaglerocklodge.com
- **Blue Spruce B&B,** Sisters, 97759, (888) 328-9644, (541) 549-9644, www.bluesprucebnb.com
- **McKenzie River Retreat B&B,** Leaburg, 97489, (541) 654-3900, (541) 896-0111, www.mckenzieriverretreat.com

TACKLE SHOPS/BOAT RENTALS

- **McKenzie Feed & Tackle,** Springfield, 97478, (541) 741-0191
- **The Fly Fisher's Place,** Sisters, 97759, (541) 549-3474, www.flyfishersplace.com

VISITOR INFORMATION

- **Linn County Parks & Recreation** (Boat Ramps), Albany, 97322, (541) 967-3917, www.linnparks.com
- **Sisters Chamber of Commerce,** Sisters, 97759, (541) 549-0251, www.sisterscountry.com
- **McKenzie River Chamber of Commerce,** Blue River, 97413, (541) 896-3330, www.mckenziechamber.com
- **Sweet Home Chamber of Commerce,** Sweet Home, 97386, (541) 367-6186, www.sweethomechamber.com

NEAREST CITIES/TOWNS

Sweet Home, 97386; McKenzie Bridge, 97413; Sisters, 97759

Best For Fishing

May–October

Other Family Activities

- Hiking
- Boating
- Camping

Amenities

Resorts	Yes
Launches	boat launch fee $5.00
Speed Limit	motors not allowed
Campgrounds	Yes
Day–Use Area	Yes
Boat Rental	$25/day

Detroit Lake

The Detroit Dam was built in 1953, creating a large water storage and electric power generation reservoir that has become an important recreation resource. This nine-mile lake, with 32 miles of shoreline, is surrounded by forest of Douglas fir and hemlock. Fed by the Breitenbush, North Fork Santiam rivers and Blowout and Kinney and several smaller creeks, it has multiple arms and a diverse coldwater fishery.

ODFW stocks Detroit Lake with between 100,000 and 120,000 legal rainbows throughout the season. Upstream, the Breitenbush and North Fork of the Santiam receive additional fish. Besides rainbows, this 3,580-acre reservoir is also home to landlocked chinook salmon and kokanee, as well as smaller populations of brook trout and cutthroat. Angling success picks up in May when the water warms.

Water-sports activity escalates in late June and trout seem to go off the bite in high-traffic areas. In the cool of morning and late evening, trout begin to feed again in earnest.

Bank access is good. From shore, fish the North Fork Santiam River, Breitenbush River, Tumble Creek and French Creek arms or fish beneath the Highway 22 Bridge or at the dam.

Most fishermen bring a boat or rent one. Trolling is popular, with flashers, four feet of leader and a spinner setup or small spoon tipped with bait. A small rainbow-pattern Rapala or a little crawdad pattern crankbait can be a good producer.

Popular trolling areas include Piety Island, west of Mongold State Park, the north shore near the dam, in front of the marinas and at the mouths of the inlets.

Illegal introductions of bullhead catfish and largemouth bass have created a new dimension to the Detroit fishery. Bullhead run 12 to 14 inches. Shallow waters on the north end of the lake and around Piety Island offer the best fishing for catfish.

LOCATION: Marion & Linn Counties

Detroit Lake, close to population centers in Portland, Salem and Bend, is a popular destination. Campgrounds, day-use areas, marinas, shopping and restaurants make it fun for the whole family.

Trout action on this popular Cascades reservoir heats up in May when water temperatures begin to climb.

VITAL STATISTICS

Surface Acres	**3580 acres**
GPS coordinates	**N 44 43.17' W 122 14.55'**
Elevation	**1569 feet above sea level**
Depth	**440 feet**

BEST FLY-FISHING TECHNIQUES

best	good	slow	Jan	Feb	Mar	Apr	May	Jun	Jul	Aug	Sep	Oct	Nov	Dec
Rainbow						2,5	2,5	2,3,5	2,3,5	2,5	2,5	2,5		
Kokanee						5,7	5,7	5,7	5,7	5,7	5,7			
Chinook						2,7	2,7	2,7	2,7	2,7	2,7	2,7		

1. Two-fly Chironomid and indicator rig
2. Weighted streamer retrieve/intermediate line leech retrieve
3. Dragonfly/damselfly nymph retrieves
4. Dry-fly dead-drift to rising trout
5. Wind drifting/trolling
6. Dry-fly with dropper nymph/Chironomid
7. Countdown method for sinking fly line

SPECIES

RB	**Rainbow trout**
Bro	**Brook trout**
CT	**Cutthroat trout**
LC	**Landlocked Chinook**
K	**Kokanee**
LB	**Largemouth bass**
BB	**Brown bullhead catfish**

BEST TROUT/KOKANEE GEAR-FISHING TECHNIQUES

best	good	slow	Jan	Feb	Mar	Apr	May	Jun	Jul	Aug	Sep	Oct	Nov	Dec
Rainbow						1,4,5,6	1,4,5,6	1,4,5,6	1,4,5,6	1,4,5,6	1,4,5,6	1,4,5,6		
Kokanee						2,8	2,8	2	2	2	2			
Chinook						1,8	1,8	1,4,8	1,4,8	1,4,8	'1,4,8	1,4,8		

1. Spinner and worm troll
2. Kokanee Wedding Ring spinner and corn troll
3. Downrigger lake trout troll
4. Casting Lures: Injured-minnow imitation; spoon; spinner
5. Sliding sinker and jar bait
6. Bobber and bait
7. Spinning-rod fly and bubble
8. Kokanee/trout jigging

AMENITIES

Resorts	**Yes**
Launches	**4**
Speed Limit	**No**
Campgrounds	**7**
Day–Use Area	**Yes**
Boat Rental	**Yes**

SERVICES

CAMPING/PARKS
- **Detroit Lake State Recreation Area**, info: (800) 551-6949, Reserve: (800) 452-5687, www.oregonstateparks.org
- **Cove Creek Campground**, Reserve: (877) 444-6777, Info: (801) 226-3564, www.reserveamerica.gov
- **Detroit Lake Marina**, Detroit, 97342, (503) 854-3423, www.detroitlakemarina.com
- **Hoover Campground**, Reserve: (877) 444-6777, www.reserveamerica.com
- **Kane's Marina**, Detroit, 97342, (503) 854-3362, www.kanesmarina.com
- **South Shore**, Detroit, 97360, (503) 854-3366, www.eatstayplay.com
- **Whispering Falls**, Detroit, 97360, (503) 854-3366, www.fs.usda.gov
- **Piety Island Campground**, Detroit, 97360, (503) 854-3366, boat-in access only, www.fs.usda.gov
- **Andrew Wiley State Park**, Sweet home, 97386, day-use only, www.recreationparks.net
- **Willamette National Forest**, (541) 225-6300, www.fs.usda.gov/willamette

ACCOMMODATIONS
- **All Seasons Motel**, Detroit, 97342, (503) 854-3421, www.allseasonsmotel.net
- **The Lodge at Detroit Lake**, Detroit, 97342, (503) 854-3344, www.lodgeatdetroitlake.com
- **Elkhorn Valley Inn**, Lyons, 97358, (503) 897-3033, (800) 707-3033, www.elkhornvalleyinnbedandbreakfast.com
- **Gardner House B&B**, Stayton, 97383, (503) 769-5478, www.gardnerhousebnb.com
- **Breitenbush Hot Springs Retreat**, Detroit, 97342, Reservations: (503) 854-3320, www.breitenbush.com

TACKLE SHOPS
- **Kanes Marina**, Detroit, 97342, (503) 854-3362, www.kanesmarina.com
- **Detroit Lake Marina**, Detroit, 97342, (503) 854-3423, www.detroitlakemarina.com
- **Rivers Run**, Detroit, 97342, (503) 854-3039
- **Mountain High Grocery**, Detroit, 97342, (503) 854-3696

VISITOR INFORMATION
- **Detroit Lake Recreation Area Business Assoc.**, www.detroitlakeoregon.org
- **Detroit Lake State Recreation Area**, Info: (800) 551-6949, Reserve: (800) 452-5687, www.oregonstateparks.org
- **Detroit Ranger Station**, Detroit, 97360, (503) 854-3366, www.fs.usda.gov

NEAREST CITIES/TOWNS
Detroit, 97342; Mill City, 97360

BEST FOR FISHING
May–October

OTHER FAMILY ACTIVITIES
- Detroit Lake Fishing Derby (May)
- Free Family Fishing Weekend (June)
- Fireworks Over the Lake (4th of July)
- Music on the Mountain Blue Grass and Gospel Jam
- 50s Cruz-In at the Lake (September)
- Snowmobile Swap Meet (November)
- Detroit Lake Area Holiday Festival
- Hiking
- Mountain biking
- Boating
- Rafting
- Swimming
- Wildlife viewing
- Nordic skiing
- Camping
- Picnicking
- Hunting
- Hot springs
- Shopping

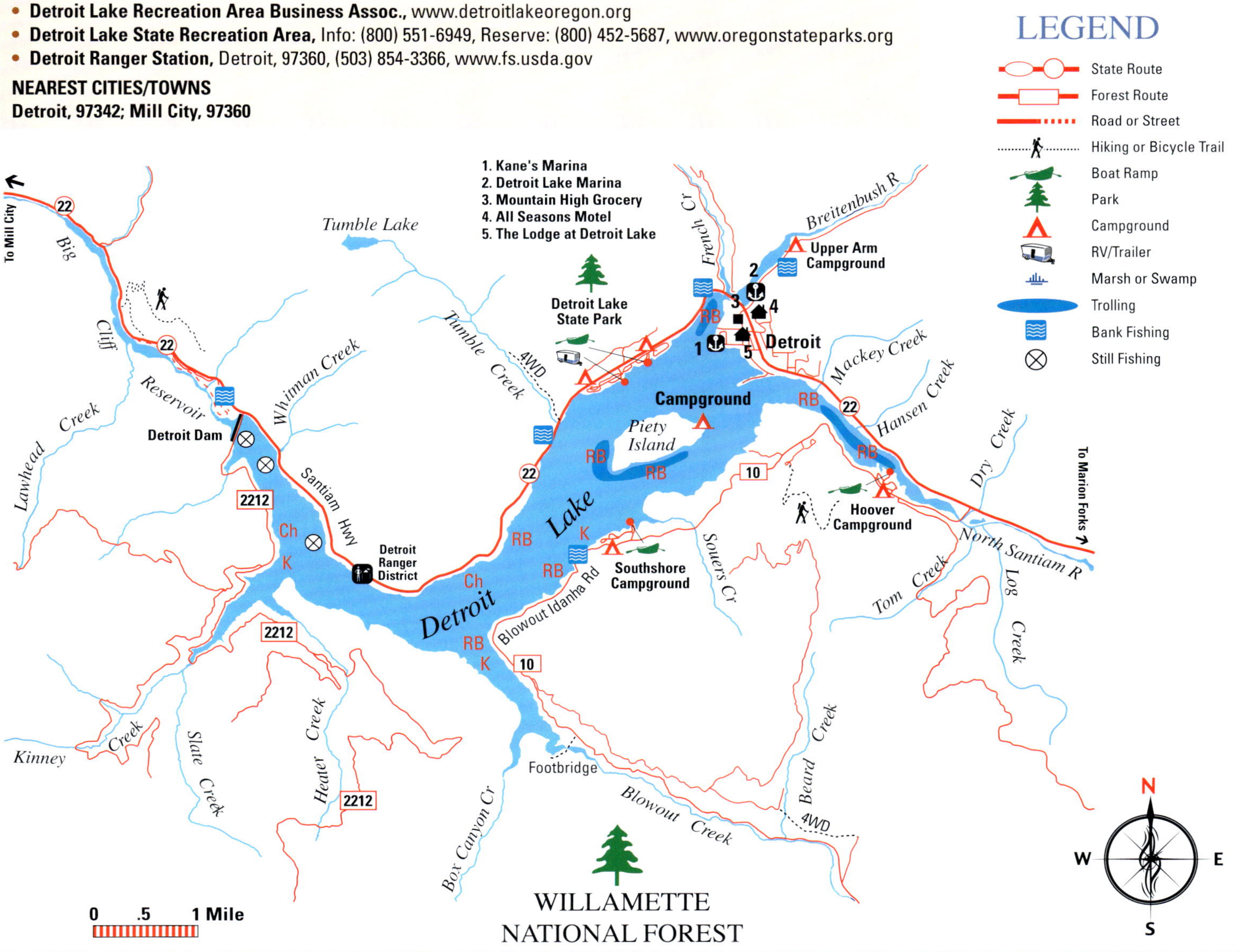

LEGEND
State Route, Forest Route, Road or Street, Hiking or Bicycle Trail, Boat Ramp, Park, Campground, RV/Trailer, Marsh or Swamp, Trolling, Bank Fishing, Still Fishing

WILLAMETTE NATIONAL FOREST

35

Fern Ridge Reservoir

LOCATION: Lane County

Photo by Gary Lewis

Fern Ridge Reservoir is a great warmwater fishery close to Eugene. This largest of the Willamette Valley lakes has well-developed parks that offer plenty of access to bank anglers and boaters alike.

At full pool, Fern Ridge Reservoir holds 9,360 surface acres of water, making it the largest lake in the Willamette Valley. This flood control reservoir was built on the Long Tom River in 1941 and has become an important recreation destination.

Fern Ridge has a maximum depth of 33 feet, but the average depth is 11 feet. Reed canary grass, bulrushes and cattails provide cover for birds and shade and feed for fish. Stands of flooded timber, riprap, old creek channels, weedbeds and many fingers and sloughs provide habitat for largemouth bass, crappie, bluegill, catfish and cutthroat trout.

Fed by several streams, the reservoir's only freshwater influence in the heat of summer is Long Tom River, which continues to flow year-round. Water level is maintained as high as possible until September, when drawdown begins. By mid-November, the lake is at its lowest point, ready to operate for flood control.

For largemouth, explore the fingers of the lake, around Gibson Island and wherever structure and topography might hold the baitfish upon which the bass feed. Bluegill are found in shallows and weeds. Find crappie along Highway 126, around Perkins Peninsula Park, near weedbeds and around the dam structure.

There are four boat launches: Richardson Park, Orchard Point Park, Fern Ridge Shores and Perkins Peninsula Park. The well-developed parks have swimming areas and picnic tables. When the water is down, the best fishing access is by the dam.

Another option is nearby Kirk Pond, a narrow lake that runs parallel to the dam on the other side of Clear Lake Road.

Sailing and kayaking are popular on Fern Ridge Reservoir. Speed restrictions are meant to keep all users happy. No motors are allowed south of Highway 126.

BEST TROUT/KOKANEE GEAR-FISHING TECHNIQUES

best	good	slow	Jan	Feb	Mar	Apr	May	Jun	Jul	Aug	Sep	Oct	Nov	Dec
Cutthroat			4	4	4	6,7	6,7	6,7	6,7	6,7	6,7	6,7	4	4

1. Spinner and worm troll
2. Kokanee Wedding Ring spinner and corn troll
3. Downrigger lake trout troll
4. Casting Lures: Injured-minnow imitation; spoon; spinner
5. Sliding sinker and jar bait
6. Bobber and bait
7. Spinning-rod fly and bubble
8. Kokanee/trout jigging

BEST FLY-FISHING TECHNIQUES

best	good	slow	Jan	Feb	Mar	Apr	May	Jun	Jul	Aug	Sep	Oct	Nov	Dec
Cutthroat			2	2	2	2	2	2	2,7	2,7	2,7	2	2	2
Crappie			2	2	2	2	2,5	2,5	2,5	2,5	2,5	2	2	2
Bluegill			1	1	1	1	1,6	1,6	1,6	1,6	1,6	1	1	1
Largemouth			2	2	2	2	2	2	2	2	2	2	2	2

1. Two-fly Chironomid and indicator rig
2. Weighted streamer retrieve/intermediate line leech retrieve
3. Dragonfly/damselfly nymph retrieves
4. Dry-fly dead-drift to rising trout
5. Wind drifting/trolling
6. Dry-fly with dropper nymph/Chironomid
7. Countdown method for sinking fly line

BEST BASS AND PANFISH TECHNIQUES

best	good	slow	Jan	Feb	Mar	Apr	May	Jun	Jul	Aug	Sep	Oct	Nov	Dec
Largemouth			3,4	3,4	3,4	1	1,7	6,7	5,6,7	2,6,7	2,6,7	2,4	3,4	3,4
Crappie			3	3	3	3	3	3	3	3	3	3	3	3
Bluegill			3	3	3	3	3	3	3	3	3	3	3	3

1. Carolina rig
2. Spinner bait
3. Crappie jig
4. Dropshot
5. Crankbait
6. Top-water plug/buzzbait
7. Senko worm rig

AMENITIES

Resorts	No
Launches	4
Speed Limit	5mph/10 mph
Campgrounds	Yes
Day–Use Area	Yes
Boat Rental	Yes

SPECIES

LB	Largemouth bass
Cr	Crappie
BL	Bluegill
BB	Brown bullhead catfish
CT	Cutthroat trout

VITAL STATISTICS

Surface Acres	9360 acres
GPS coordinates	N 44 03.171' W 123 17.506'
Elevation	374 feet above sea level
Depth	33 feet

BEST FOR FISHING

May–October

OTHER FAMILY ACTIVITIES

- Boating
- Parks
- Wineries
- Oregon Country Fair (Veneta, July)
- Scandinavian Festival (Junction City, August)
- Lane County Fair (Eugene, August)
- Cities of Veneta & Junction City
- Downtown Eugene
- Covered Bridges
- University of Oregon
- Mount Pisgah Arboretum
- Hunting
- Hiking
- Golfing
- Wildlife viewing
- Birding
- Swimming
- Picnicking

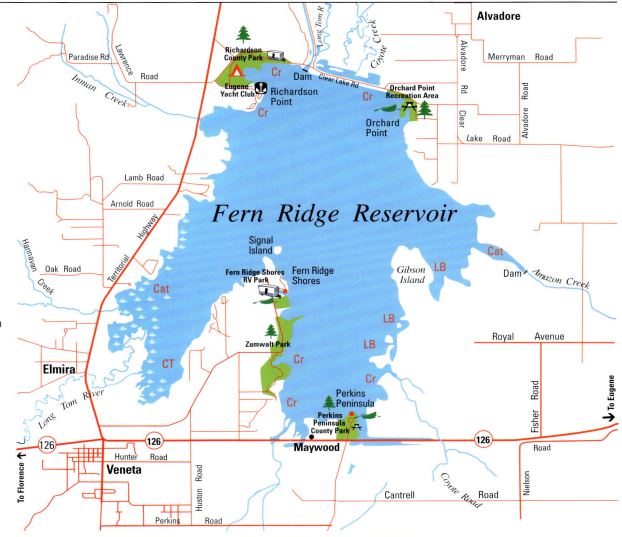

SERVICES

CAMPING & PARKS

- **Fern Ridge Shores,** Veneta, 97487, (541) 935-2335, www.fernridgeshores.com
- **Kirk Park,** (541) 688-8147, day-use only, www.lanecounty.org
- **Orchard Point Park,** (541) 688-8147, day-use only, www.lanecounty.org
- **Perkins Peninsula Park,** (541) 688-8147, day-use only, www.lanecounty.org
- **Richardson Park,** Reserve: (541) 682-2000, www.lanecounty.org
- **Zumwalt Park,** (541) 682-2000, day-use only, www.lanecounty.org

ACCOMMODATIONS

- **The Catbird Seat B&B,** Junction City, 97448, (541) 953-7851, www.thecatbirdseatbandb.com
- **Augusta House B&B,** Eugene, 97405, (541) 513-5593, www.augustahouse.net
- **C'est La Vie Inn,** Eugene, 97402, (866) 302-3014, (541) 302-3014, www.cestlavieinn.com

TACKLE SHOPS/BOAT RENTALS

- **Home Waters Fly Fishing,** Eugene, 97401, (541) 342-6691, www.eugeneflyshop.com
- **The Caddis Fly Angling Shop,** Eugene, 97401, (541) 342-7005, www.thecaddisfly.com
- **Dick's Sporting Goods,** Eugene, 97408, (541) 344-9622, www.dickssportinggoods.com
- **Sports Authority,** Eugene, 97401, (541) 342-2066, www.sportsauthority.com
- **Mazama Sporting Goods/Fishing Pro Shop,** Eugene, 97402, (541) 357-4419, www.mazamasportinggoods.com
- **Oregon Rod Reel & Tackle,** Eugene, 97408, (541) 683-4965, www.oregonrrt.com

VISITOR INFORMATION

- **Eugene Area Chamber of Commerce,** Eugene, 97401, (541) 484-1314, www.eugenechamber.com
- **Fern Ridge Chamber of Commerce,** Veneta, 97487, (541) 935-8443, www.fernridgechamber.com
- **Lane County Parks,** Eugene, 97408, (541) 682-2000, www.lanecounty.org
- **Lane County Parks Reservation,** Eugene, 97408, (541) 682-2000, www.reservations.lanecounty.org

NEAREST CITIES/TOWNS

Eugene, 97401-97408, 97412, 97440; Veneta, 97487

LEGEND

 State Route

 Road or Street

 Boat Ramp

 Park

 Campground

RV/Trailer

Marsh or Swamp

0   .5   1 Mile

Green Peter Reservoir

Green Peter Reservoir, on the Middle Santiam River, is located east of Sweet Home and north of Highway 20. Completed in 1968, this 3700-acre reservoir boasts a big population of kokanee and rainbow trout, as well as landlocked chinook, largemouth bass, crappie and bluegill. At full pool, the lake is ten miles long and has a shoreline 38 miles long. Boat ramps are found at Thistle Creek and Whitcomb Creek Park.

The Oregon Department of Fish and Wildlife stocks the lake with rainbows and chinook. This lake fishes well throughout spring and summer, but some of the best days come early and late in the season. As stocked trout disperse throughout the lake in summer, they seek out cooler water of Santiam and the mouths of its tributary creeks: Whitcomb, Quartzville, Tally and Rumbaugh and others.

Bank fishermen can catch trout with nightcrawlers and jar baits near the creek mouths, at the dam and at stocking points (boat ramps). But because of the patchwork of private land and limited, steep bank access in most places, trolling is the most popular method for trout anglers.

Some of the best kokanee spots are by the dam, in the Quartzville arm and around the peninsula in the main channel. For kokanee, jigging is a favorite technique early in the year, but trollers seem to do better in summer. An easy rig, whether using a downrigger or not, consists of an eight-inch flasher on the main line with four feet of leader terminated at an Apex or Wedding Ring spinner. Most anglers add white corn and season it by adding a scent like Pautzke's Krill.

Shoreline grasses, flooded timber and other structure hold largemouth bass and crappie, especially in the middle Santiam arm.

Water fluctuates from spring to fall. The water stratifies in summer and the intakes for the power plant are deep to pump cooler water into the river below the dam.

Campground ponds are stocked with trout in advance of Free Fishing Day in June. Nearby, you'll find Foster Reservoir, a 1200-acre lake that holds back the South and Middle forks of the Santiam. Rainbows are stocked in April and May.

At Green Peter, trolling is one of the most popular techniques to put a limit of kokanee or hatchery rainbows in the boat. Mikayla Lewis (left) and Adrienne Luoma celebrate a fat koke they caught on trolling gear.

LOCATION: Linn County

AMENITIES

Resorts	No
Launches	2
Speed Limit	No
Campgrounds	3
Day–Use Areas	Shea Point, Andrew S. Wiley Park

SERVICES

CAMPING & PARKS
- **Whitcomb Creek County Park,** (541) 967-3917, Reserve: www.linnparks.com
- **Lynchwood City Park,** Cascadia, 97329
- **Thistle Creek Boat Ramp,** (541) 967-3917, www.linnparks.com
- **Sunnyside County Park,** Foster, 97345, (541) 967-3917, www.linnparks.com

ACCOMMODATIONS
- **Historic CJ Howe Building Vacation Loft,** Brownsville, 97327, (541) 466-9109, www.cjhowebuilding.com
- **The Hanson Country Inn,** Corvallis, 97333, (541) 752-2919, www.hcinn.com
- **The Catbird Seat B&B,** Junction City, 97448, (541) 953-7851, www.thecatbirdseatbandb.com
- **Gardner House B&B,** Stayton, 97383, (503) 769-5478, www.gardnerhousebnb.com

TACKLE SHOPS/BOAT RENTALS
- **Two Rivers Fly Shop,** Albany, 97321, (800) 373-9289, (541) 967-9800, www.tworiversflyshop.biz
- **Xtreme Northwest Bait Co.,** Lebanon, 97355, (541) 981-4449, www.xtremenorthwest.com
- **Big 5 Sporting Goods,** Albany, 97321, (541) 926-7273, www.big5sportinggoods.com

VISITOR INFORMATION
- **Linn County Parks & Recreation** (boat ramps), Albany, 97332, (541) 967-3917, www.linnparks.com
- **Sweet Home Chamber Of Commerce,** 97386, (541) 367-6186, www.sweethomechamber.com
- **Covered Bridge Society of Oregon,** www.covered-bridges.org

NEAREST CITIES/TOWNS
Sweet Home, 97386

SPECIES

RB	Rainbow trout
K	Kokanee
Ch	Chinook
LB	Largemouth bass
Cr	Crappie
BL	Bluegill

BEST FOR FISHING
April–October

OTHER FAMILY ACTIVITIES
- Waterskiing
- Picnicking
- Camping
- Swimming
- Hiking (Whitcomb Creek Park)

BEST BASS AND PANFISH TECHNIQUES

best	good	slow	Jan	Feb	Mar	Apr	May	Jun	Jul	Aug	Sep	Oct	Nov	Dec
Largemouth						1,7	1,7	2,4,5	2,4,5	2,6,7	2,6,7	2,5		
Crappie							3	3	3	3	3			
Bluegill							3	3	3	3	3			

1. Carolina rig
2. Spinner bait
3. Crappie jig
4. Dropshot
5. Crankbait
6. Top-water plug/buzzbait
7. Senko worm rig

BEST TROUT/KOKANEE GEAR-FISHING TECHNIQUES

best	good	slow	Jan	Feb	Mar	Apr	May	Jun	Jul	Aug	Sep	Oct	Nov	Dec
Rainbow						1,4,6	1,4,5,6	1,4,5	1,5,8	1,5	5	5		
Kokanee						2,8	2,8	2,8	2	2	2			

1. Spinner and worm troll
2. Kokanee Wedding Ring spinner and corn troll
3. Downrigger lake trout troll
4. Casting Lures: Injured-minnow imitation; spoon; spinner
5. Sliding sinker and jar bait
6. Bobber and bait
7. Spinning-rod fly and bubble
8. Kokanee/trout jigging

LEGEND

- State Route
- Forest Route
- Road or Street
- Hiking or Bicycle Trail
- Boat Ramp
- Park
- Campground
- RV/Trailer
- Trolling
- Bank Fishing

0   .5   1 Mile

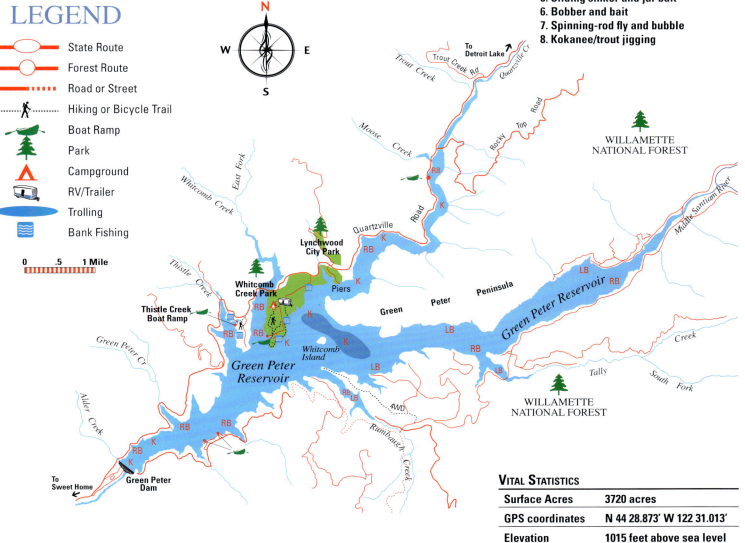

VITAL STATISTICS

Surface Acres	3720 acres
GPS coordinates	N 44 28.873' W 122 31.013'
Elevation	1015 feet above sea level
Depth	315 feet

BEST FLY-FISHING TECHNIQUES

best	good	slow	Jan	Feb	Mar	Apr	May	Jun	Jul	Aug	Sep	Oct	Nov	Dec
Rainbow						1,2,5	1,2,3,5	1,2,3,4	1,3,7	1,3,7	1,4	1,2		
Kokanee						5,7	5,7	5,7	5,7	5,7	5,7			

1. Two-fly Chironomid and indicator rig
2. Weighted streamer retrieve/ intermediate line leech retrieve
3. Dragonfly/damselfly nymph retrieves
4. Dry-fly dead-drift to rising trout
5. Wind drifting/trolling
6. Dry-fly with dropper nymph/Chironomid
7. Countdown method for sinking fly line

Henry Hagg Lake

Southwest of Hillsboro, the US Bureau of Reclamation's Henry Hagg Lake provides one of the best early-season opportunities for Portland-area anglers. This water-storage reservoir was built to control flooding in the Tualatin watershed. It has become a great smallmouth bass and trout fishery.

The best trout action is from March through June. Abundant rainbows (ODFW stocks 60,000 legal fish a year), smallmouth bass, and perch make it an interesting fishery. Rainbow trout average ten inches, but can grow beyond five pounds in this food-rich water.

For early season anglers, ODFW plants 9,000 legal rainbows at the end of February and will put at least that many more in the water by the end of March.

Prospect for trout in the Scoggins Creek arm on the west shore. From a boat, try trolling along the channel between the Scoggins Creek arm toward Boat Ramp C. Rig with a Ford Fender lake troll. Use a nickel finish in clear water and brass or copper in off-colored water. Behind the lake troll, tie on four feet of six-pound-test leader terminated at a small Dick Nite spoon. Tip the hook with a piece of nightcrawler.

Troll no faster than one mile per hour. If it takes dragging a bucket or sea anchor to slow the boat down, do it. The key to success when trolling is to keep your speed down. The thump of the blade should be slow, the spoon wobbling, not spinning. Vary the speed, depth and direction to spark strikes from following fish.

Bass fishing turns on when the water temperature approaches 60 degrees. Hagg Lake holds the state record for smallmouth bass, a fish that weighed 7 pounds, 14 ounces. If the record is broken again, there is a good chance it will come from Hagg Lake. The Tanner Creek and Sain Creek arms are good bets for smallies. The dam face and the overlook can produce smallmouth or largemouth bass.

The park is open sunrise to sunset the first Saturday of March through the Sunday before Thanksgiving. A vehicle daily pass costs $5.00 and a vehicle with boat pass costs $6.00. Season passes are available.

Photo by Gary Lewis

One of the most productive waters in western Oregon, Henry Hagg Lake is a short drive from the most populous corner of the state. The lake is famous for big bass and fat rainbows.

LOCATION: Washington County

VITAL STATISTICS

Surface Acres	1153 acres
GPS coordinates	N 45 28.189' W 123 12.263'
Elevation	304 feet above sea level
Depth	110 feet

SERVICES

CAMPING & PARKS
- **Brown's Camp,** (503) 357-2191, www.oregon.gov
- **Hagg Lake Park,** Gaston, 97119, (503) 359-5732, www.co.washington.or.us
- **Tillamook State Forest,** (503) 815-6800, (503) 359-7402, www.oregon.gov

ACCOMMODATIONS
- **Cottage in the Grove,** Forest Grove, 97116, (503) 201-3775, www.cottageinthegrove.com
- **Yamhill Vineyards B&B**, Yamhill, 97148, (503) 662-3840, www.yamhillvineyardsbb.com

TACKLE SHOPS/BOAT RENTALS
- **Lunch Express and Boat Rental,** Gaston, 97119, (503) 927-5489
- **Big 5 Sporting Goods,** Hillsboro, 97123, (503) 681-0364, www.big5sportinggoods.com
- **Dick's Sporting Goods,** Hillsboro, 97124, (503) 547-2904, www.dickssportinggoods.com

VISITOR INFORMATION
- **Forest Grove/Cornelius Chamber Of Commerce,** Forest Grove, 97116, (503) 357-3006, visitforestgrove.com
- **Washington County,** Hillsboro, 97124, (503) 846-8611, www.co.washington.or.us
- **City of Forest Grove,** Forest Grove, 97116, (503) 992-3200, www.forestgrove-or.gov
- **Tree to Tree Aerial Adventure Park,** Gaston, 97119, (503) 357-0109, www.tree2treeadventurepark.com

NEAREST CITIES/TOWNS
Gaston, 97119; Forest Grove, 97116

AMENITIES

Resorts	No
Launches	2
Speed Limit	35mph
Campgrounds	No
Day–Use Area	Yes
Boat Rental	No

SPECIES

RB	Rainbow trout
CT	Cutthroat trout
SB	Smallmouth bass
LB	Largemouth bass
Cr	Crappie
YP	Yellow perch
BL	Bluegill

BEST FLY-FISHING TECHNIQUES

best	good	slow	Jan	Feb	Mar	Apr	May	Jun	Jul	Aug	Sep	Oct	Nov	Dec
Rainbow					2,5	2,5	2,3,5	2,3,5	1,2,7	1,2,7	2,5	2,5		
Crappie					2	2	2	2	2	2	2	2		
Bluegill					6	6	6	6	6	6	6	6		
Bass					2,7	2,7	2,7	2,7	2,7	2,7	2,7	2,7		

1. Two-fly Chironomid and indicator rig
2. Weighted streamer retrieve/ intermediate line leech retrieve
3. Dragonfly/damselfly nymph retrieves
4. Dry-fly dead-drift to rising trout
5. Wind drifting/trolling
6. Dry-fly with dropper nymph/Chironomid
7. Countdown method for sinking fly line

BEST BASS AND PANFISH TECHNIQUES

best	good	slow	Jan	Feb	Mar	Apr	May	Jun	Jul	Aug	Sep	Oct	Nov	Dec
Largemouth					1,4	1,4	1,4	1,7	1,6,7	1,6,7	2,5	2,5		
Smallmouth					1,4	1,4	1,4	1,7	1,6,7	1,6,7	2,5	2,5		
Crappie					3	3	3	3	3	3	3	3		
Bluegill					3	3	3	3	3	3	3	3		

1. Carolina rig
2. Spinner bait
3. Crappie jig
4. Dropshot
5. Crankbait
6. Top-water plug/buzzbait
7. Senko worm rig

BEST TROUT/KOKANEE GEAR-FISHING TECHNIQUES

best	good	slow	Jan	Feb	Mar	Apr	May	Jun	Jul	Aug	Sep	Oct	Nov	Dec
Rainbow					1,6,8	1,6,8	1,5,6	1,5,6	1,5,6	1,5,6	1,5,8	1,5,8		

1. Spinner and worm troll
2. Kokanee Wedding Ring spinner and corn troll
3. Downrigger lake trout troll
4. Casting Lures: Injured-minnow imitation; spoon; spinner
5. Sliding sinker and jar bait
6. Bobber and bait
7. Spinning-rod fly and bubble
8. Kokanee/trout jigging

BEST FOR FISHING

March–June,

September–October

OTHER FAMILY ACTIVITIES

• Hiking
• Wildlife watching
• Birding
• Picnicking
• Swimming
• Mountain biking
• Disabled–visitor facilities

LEGEND

━━━ ‥‥‥ Road or Street

Boat Ramp

Park

Trolling

Bank Fishing

⊗ Still Fishing

0 .5 1 Mile

North Fork Reservoir

Photo by Gary Lewis

This long, narrow reservoir is a favorite trolling destination, but there is good bank angling to be found on the north shore.

LOCATION: Clackamas County

VITAL STATISTICS

Surface Acres	324 acres
GPS coordinates	N 45 13.406' W 122 14.866'
Elevation	665 feet above sea level
Depth	120 feet

Construction of the 207-foot-high dam at the confluence of the North Fork and the mainstem Clackamas was finished in 1958, creating North Fork Reservoir. This narrow, deep, electrical-power-generation pool stretches four miles into the western slope of the Cascades.

Much of the shoreline is private, but undeveloped. The topography is rugged, with older volcanic flows carved by inlet streams. Above the lake, the ground rises steeply, and is densely forested with Douglas firs.

Within easy driving distance of Portland, North Fork Reservoir is a popular destination for boaters, waterskiers and fishermen. There is some native fish production, but angling efforts are concentrated on hatchery fish. ODFW stocks close to 80,000 legal rainbows from May through September. Only adipose-fin-clipped trout may be retained. Wild rainbows, cutthroat, brook trout, brown trout and bull trout must be released.

The best fishing is found in the faster water at the upper end of the lake, near the marina and at the boat launches. Popular trolling areas include the log boom in front of the dam, the north shore, near the lower launch and under the power lines.

Good bank fishing can be found at the wheelchair-accessible ramp, the log booms, near the North Fork inlet and close to the boat launches.

Groceries, fishing tackle, and boat and motor rentals are available at the concession store located at Promontory Park. A boat dock and launching area are next to the store.

For people with disabilities, the park has an accessible restroom, campsites, boat dock and rentable patio boats.

There is no speed limit on the lower half of the reservoir, but the upper half has a 10-mph speed limit.

Nearby, the one-acre Small Fry Pond is a great place to take kids for a chance at a 'keeper.' Fishing at Small Fry is limited to kids aged 14-years and under. There is a three-fish limit.

BEST TROUT/KOKANEE GEAR-FISHING TECHNIQUES

best	good	slow	Jan	Feb	Mar	Apr	May	Jun	Jul	Aug	Sep	Oct	Nov	Dec
Rainbow							1,5,8	1,5,6,7	1,5,6,7	1,5	1,5,6	1,5,6		

1. Spinner and worm troll
2. Kokanee Wedding Ring spinner and corn troll
3. Downrigger lake trout troll
4. Casting Lures: Injured-minnow imitation; spoon; spinner
5. Sliding sinker and jar bait
6. Bobber and bait
7. Spinning-rod fly and bubble
8. Kokanee/trout jigging

BEST FLY-FISHING TECHNIQUES

best	good	slow	Jan	Feb	Mar	Apr	May	Jun	Jul	Aug	Sep	Oct	Nov	Dec
Rainbow							2,5	2,5	2,5,7	2,5,7	2,5	2,5		

1. Two-fly chironomid and indicator rig
2. Weighted streamer retrieve/intermediate line leech retrieve
3. Dragonfly/damselfly nymph retrieves
4. Dry fly dead drift to rising trout
5. Wind drifting/trolling
6. Dry-fly with dropper nymph/chironomid
7. Countdown method for sinking fly line

SPECIES

RB	**Rainbow trout**
CT	**Cutthroat trout**
BTr	**Bull trout**
Bro	**Brook trout**
BT	**Brown trout**

AMENITIES

Resorts	**No**
Launches	**3**
Speed Limit	**No**
Campgrounds	**Yes**
Day–Use Area	**Yes**
Boat Rental	**Yes**

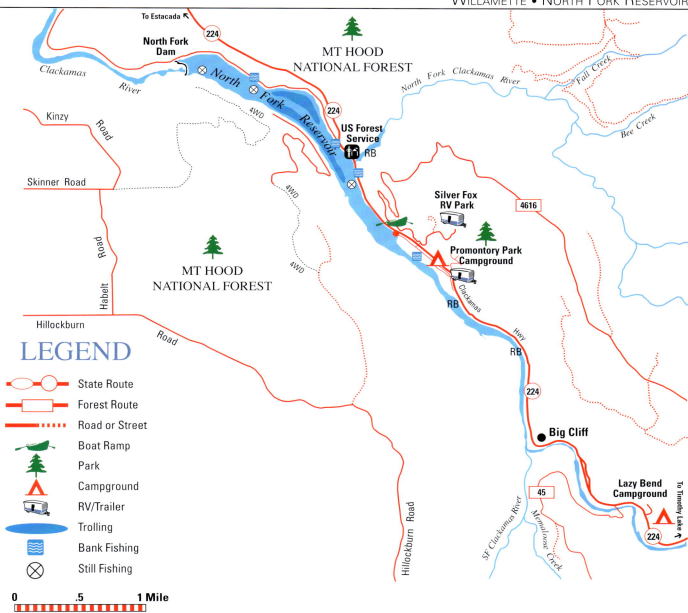

LEGEND

⬭—⬤	State Route
▭	Forest Route
▬▬ ⋯	Road or Street
🛶	Boat Ramp
🌲	Park
⛺	Campground
🚐	RV/Trailer
⬯	Trolling
≋	Bank Fishing
⊗	Still Fishing

0   .5   1 Mile

SERVICES

CAMPING & PARKS
- **Promontory Park Campground,** Estacada, 97023, (503) 630-7229, www.portlandgeneral.com
- **Lazy Bend Campground,** Estacada, 97023, Reserve: (877) 444-6777, www.fs.usda.gov
- **Silver Fox RV Park,** Estacada, 97023, (503) 630-7000, www.silverfoxrvpark.com

ACCOMMODATIONS
- **Sandy Salmon B&B Lodge,** Sandy, 97055, (503) 622-6699, www.sandysalmon.com
- **Best Western Sandy Inn,** Sandy, 97055, (503) 668-7100, www.bestwestern.com

TACKLE SHOPS/BOAT RENTALS
- **Promontory Park Store & Marina,** (503) 630-5152
- **Estacada Tackle Shop,** Estacada, 97023, (503) 630-7424,

VISITOR INFORMATION
- **Mt. Hood National Forest,** Government Camp, 97028, (503) 668-1700, www.fs.usda.gov/mthood
- **Zigzag Ranger Station,** Zigzag, 97049, (503) 622-3191, www.fs.usda.gov
- **Estacada Chamber of Commerce,** Estacada, OR 97023, (503) 630-3483, www.estacadachamber.org
- **Mt. Hood Area Chamber of Commerce,** Welches, 97067, (503) 622-3017, www.mthoodchamber.com
- **PGE Parks,** Info: (503) 464-8515, Reserve: (877) 444-6777, www.portlandgeneral.com/Community_Environment

NEAREST CITIES/TOWNS
Sandy, 97055; Estacada, 97023

BEST FOR FISHING
May–October

OTHER FAMILY ACTIVITIES
- Boating
- Camping
- Picnicking
- Hiking
- Hunting

Olallie Lake

High in the Cascades, near the headwaters of the Clackamas, you'll find Olallie Lake, nestled in a pocket of noble fir, Pacific silver fir, white pine, western hemlock, lodgepole pine and mountain hemlock. With a stunning view of the north side of Mt. Jefferson, Olallie is a favorite destination for anglers and their families.

The largest of 200 lakes in and around Olallie Butte, this lake is famous for its trophy trout. Snowpack limits access early in the season, but fishing is good when you can make it through.

Hatchery rainbows average 12 to 14 inches, but the big brood trout are what make the long drive worthwhile. Olallie regularly produces trophy trout in the 8- to 10-pound class. With numerous points and rocky outcroppings, the lake is easy to read and almost one-third of the lake is less than 10 feet deep.

Most anglers fish Olallie between June and July, but good fishing can continue through October. No motors are allowed on the lake, but trolling is popular here. Float- tubers wind-drift with flies and rowboaters pull flashers and worm gear. Bank anglers cast Rooster Tail spinners or use jar baits.

One of the most popular bank angling spots is located close to the road near the resort, where a big rock wall slopes down to the water.

There are three campgrounds on the lake and several others close by. Take care to secure food in vehicles instead of tents. A few black bears patrol the campgrounds, looking for easy meals. Marshy meadows are breeding grounds for mosquitoes. Bring repellent. Olallie's fishing is great, but the angling can be good on nearby lakes as well.

Several hiking trails pass through the area, Pacific Crest Trail, a trail to Olallie Butte, and another to Twin Peaks. A trail also encircles the lake. Olallie is a Chinook word for berries. Huckleberries can be found in late August and September.

This is one of Oregon's top lakes for producing big rainbows. There is some bank angling, but the best be is to bring a boat or rent one from the resort. Both fly-fishing and gear are productive. Some of the bes fishing can be found in October.

LOCATION: Jefferson County

SERVICES

CAMPING & PARKS
- **Peninsula Campground,** Mt Hood National Forest, Government Camp, 97028, (503) 630-6861, www.fs.usda.gov/mthood
- **Detroit Lake State Recreation Area,** Info: (800) 551-6949, Reserve: (800) 452-5687, www.oregonstateparks.org

ACCOMMODATIONS
- **Olallie Lake Resort,** email: olallielakeresort@gmail.com, www.olallielakeresort.com

TACKLE SHOPS/BOAT RENTALS
- **Promontory Park Store & Marina,** (503) 630-5152
- **Estacada Tackle Shop,** Estacada, 97023, (503) 630-7424
- **Olallie Lake Resort Tackle & Boat Rental,** email: olallielakeresort@gmail.com, www.olallielakeresort.com
- **Kanes Marina,** Detroit, 97342, (503) 854-3362, www.kanesmarina.com
- **Detroit Lake Marina,** Detroit, 97342, (503) 854-3423, www.detroitlakemarina.com

- **The Fly Fishing Shop,** Welches, 97067, (800) 266-3971, (503) 622-4607, www.flyfishusa.com

VISITOR INFORMATION
- **Mt. Hood National Forest,** Government Camp, 97028, (503) 668-1700, www.fs.usda.gov/mthood
- **Estacada Chamber of Commerce,** Estacada, 97023, (503) 630-3483, www.estacadachamber.org
- **Mt. Hood Area Chamber of Commerce,** Welches, 97067, (503) 622-3017, www.mthoodchamber.com
- **Zigzag Ranger Station,** Zigzag, 97049, (503) 622-3191, www.fs.usda.gov
- **Detroit Ranger Station,** Detroit, 97360, (503) 854-3366, www.fs.usda.gov
- **Detroit Lake Recreation Area Business Assoc.,** www.detroitlakeoregon.org

NEAREST CITIES/TOWNS
Government Camp, 97028; Estacada, 97023; Detroit, 97342

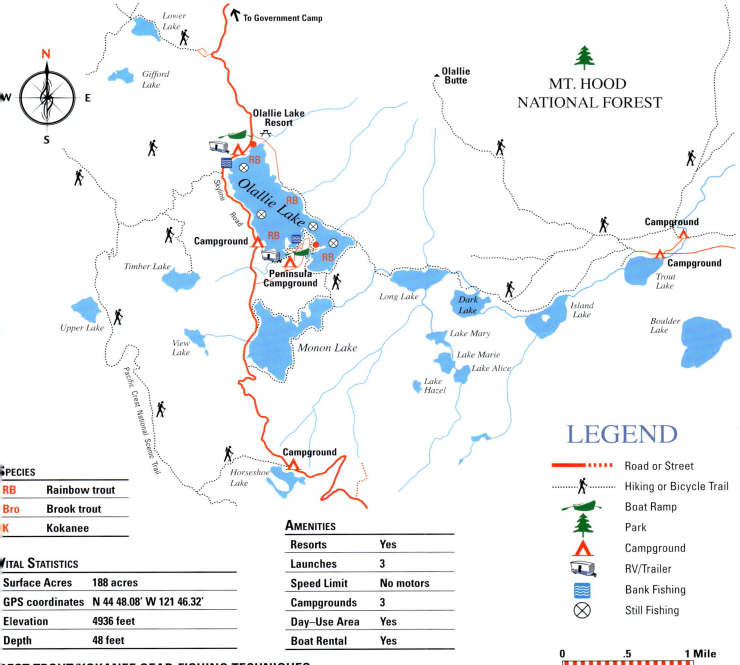

SPECIES

RB	Rainbow trout
Bro	Brook trout
K	Kokanee

VITAL STATISTICS

Surface Acres	188 acres
GPS coordinates	N 44 48.08′ W 121 46.32′
Elevation	4936 feet
Depth	48 feet

AMENITIES

Resorts	Yes
Launches	3
Speed Limit	No motors
Campgrounds	3
Day–Use Area	Yes
Boat Rental	Yes

LEGEND

Road or Street
Hiking or Bicycle Trail
Boat Ramp
Park
Campground
RV/Trailer
Bank Fishing
Still Fishing

0 — .5 — 1 Mile

BEST FOR FISHING

June–October

OTHER FAMILY ACTIVITIES

• Hiking Pacific Crest Trail
• Wildlife watching
• Huckleberry picking
• Boating
• Camping
• Picnicking
• Birding

BEST TROUT/KOKANEE GEAR-FISHING TECHNIQUES

best	good	slow	Jan	Feb	Mar	Apr	May	Jun	Jul	Aug	Sep	Oct	Nov	Dec
Rainbow							1,4,5	1,4,5	1,5,7	1,5,7	1,5	1,5		
Brook							5	5,7	5,7	5,7	5,7	5		

1. Spinner and worm troll
2. Kokanee Wedding Ring spinner and corn troll
3. Downrigger lake trout troll
4. Casting Lures: Injured-minnow imitation; spoon; spinner
5. Sliding sinker and jar bait
6. Bobber and bait
7. Spinning-rod fly and bubble
8. Kokanee/trout jigging

BEST FLY-FISHING TECHNIQUES

best	good	slow	Jan	Feb	Mar	Apr	May	Jun	Jul	Aug	Sep	Oct	Nov	Dec
Rainbow							2,7	2,5,7	1,2,5	1,2,5	2,5,7	2,7		
Brook							2,7	2,5,7	1,2,5	1,2,5	2,5,7	2,7		

1. Two-fly Chironomid and indicator rig
2. Weighted streamer retrieve/intermediate line leech retrieve
3. Dragonfly/damselfly nymph retrieves
4. Dry-fly dead-drift to rising trout
5. Wind drifting/trolling
6. Dry-fly with dropper nymph/Chironomid
7. Countdown method for sinking fly line

Lake Harriet

Lake Harriet, a 23-acre reservoir on the Oak Grove Fork of the Clackamas, has become well-known for trophy browns, rainbows, cutthroats and brook trout. The upper end of the lake is best for bigger fish, especially early and late in the day. Two boat launches make access easy and bank anglers set up along the upper north shore. The size of the lake makes it ideal for rafts, canoes and float tubes. The best fishing is near the top of the lake.

Bank anglers prefer worms fished on a sliding sinker. Some use jar baits or salmon eggs to good effect. Try Rooster Tail spinners early and late in the day.

Fly-fishermen do as well or better here than bait-anglers. But the best fly-fishing is from a boat. The flooded timber makes this lake food-rich with plenty of structure and character. The head of the lake has a riffle, pools and islands like a river. Trout feed all day in the three- to five-foot water around stumps and floating logs. Shadows concentrate the fish. A riffle on the water encourages them to elevate toward the surface.

Midge, mayfly, caddis, stonefly, damsel and dragonfly hatches may occur throughout the season. Flying ants are another summer and fall food source.

LOCATION: Clackamas County

Take Hwy 224 from Estacada into Mt. Hood National Forest. About a mile past Ripplebrook Ranger Station follow Forest Rd. 57 toward Timothy Lake. After about 6 miles, Rd. 57 crosses Oak Grove Fork. Take Forest Rd 4630 west one mile to Harriet Lake.

The Oak Grove Fork of the Clackamas is one of the only fisheries in the state where you can catch and keep cutthroat trout. Fishing is limited to flies and lures only and presents a special challenge for streamer fishermen.

This long, narrow reservoir is a favorite with bank anglers and gear-fishermen. For the best fly-rod action, bring a boat or float tube.

BEST TROUT/KOKANEE GEAR-FISHING TECHNIQUES

best good slow	Jan	Feb	Mar	Apr	May	Jun	Jul	Aug	Sep	Oct	Nov	Dec
Rainbow				4,5,6	4,5,6	4,5,7	4,5,7	5,7	5,7	5,6,7		
Brown				4,7,8	4,7,8	4,7	4,7	4,7	4,7,8	4,7,8		
Cutthroat				4,5,6	4,5,6	4,5,7	4,5,7	5,7	5,7	5,6,7		

1. Spinner and worm troll
2. Kokanee Wedding Ring spinner and corn troll
3. Downrigger lake trout troll
4. Casting Lures: Injured-minnow imitation; spoon; spinner
5. Sliding sinker and jar bait
6. Bobber and bait
7. Spinning-rod fly and bubble
8. Kokanee/trout jigging

BEST FLY-FISHING TECHNIQUES

best good slow	Jan	Feb	Mar	Apr	May	Jun	Jul	Aug	Sep	Oct	Nov	Dec
Rainbow				2,3	2,3,4	2,3,4	2,3,4,5	2,4,5	1,4,5	1,4,5		
Brown				2	2	2,7	2,7	2,7	2,7	2,7		
Cutthroat				2	2,3,5	2,3,5	2	2	2	2		

1. Two-fly Chironomid and indicator rig
2. Weighted streamer retrieve/ intermediate line leech retrieve
3. Dragonfly/damselfly nymph retrieves
4. Dry-fly dead-drift to rising trout
5. Wind drifting/trolling
6. Dry- fly with dropper nymph/Chironomid
7. Countdown method for sinking fly line

SERVICES

CAMPING & PARKS
- **Lake Harriet Campground & Boat Ramp,** Info: (503) 668-1700, Reserve: (877) 444-6777, www.fs.usda.gov
- **Lazy Bend Campground,** Estacada, 97023, Info: (503) 668-1700, Reserve: (877) 444-6777, www.fs.usda.gov

ACCOMMODATIONS
- **Sandy Salmon B&B Lodge,** Sandy, 97055, (503) 622-6699, www.sandysalmon.com
- **Best Western Sandy Inn,** Sandy, 97055, (503) 668-7100, www.bestwestern.com

TACKLE SHOPS/BOAT RENTALS
- **Estacada Tackle Shop,** Estacada, 97023, (503) 630-7424
- **The Fly Fishing Shop,** Welches, 97067, (800) 266-3971, (503) 622-4607, www.flyfishusa.com

VISITOR INFORMATION
- **Mt. Hood National Forest,** Government Camp, 97028, (503) 668-1700, www.fs.usda.gov/mthood
- **Estacada Chamber of Commerce,** Estacada, 97023, (503) 630-3483, www.estacadachamber.org
- **Mt. Hood Area Chamber of Commerce,** Welches, 97067, (503) 622-3017, www.mthoodchamber.com
- **Zigzag Ranger Station,** Zigzag, 97049, (503) 622-3191, www.fs.usda.gov

NEAREST CITIES/TOWNS
Sandy, 97055; Estacada, 97023

BEST FOR FISHING
May–October

OTHER FAMILY ACTIVITIES
- Camping
- Picnicking
- Waterfalls

AMENITIES

Resorts	No
Launches	Two
Speed Limit	No motors
Campgrounds	Yes
Day-Use Area	Yes
Boat Rental	No

SPECIES

RB	**Rainbow trout**
BT	**Brown trout**
CT	**Cutthroat trout**
Bro	**Brook trout**

VITAL STATISTICS

Surface Acres	23 acres
GPS coordinates	N 45 04.420' W 121 57.567'
Elevation	2037 feet
Depth	deepest near dam

LEGEND

▭	Forest Route
▬ ┈	Road or Street
	Boat Ramp
🌲	Park
⛺	Campground
〰	Bank Fishing

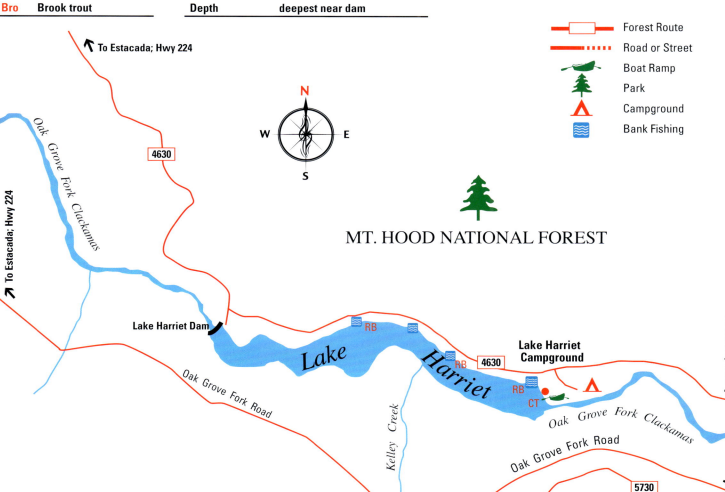

To Estacada; Hwy 224

Oak Grove Fork Clackamas

To Estacada; Hwy 224

4630

N
W · E
S

MT. HOOD NATIONAL FOREST

Lake Harriet Dam

Lake Harriet

RB

Oak Grove Fork Road

Kelley Creek

4630

RB

RB

CT

Lake Harriet Campground

Oak Grove Fork Clackamas

Oak Grove Fork Road

5730

To Timothy Lake

To Timothy Lake

0 .5 1 Mile

Lost Lake
(Hood Watershed)

Photo by Gary Lewis

A little off the beaten path, Lost Lake, in the Hood River watershed, is worth the trip for a chance to do battle with big rainbows and browns.

The Indians called it Heart of the Mountains, and it was a favorite camping area then as it is now. Today, we call it Lost Lake, but this popular 231-acre stillwater is discovered every season by travelers from all over northwest Oregon.

Surrounded by rhododendrons and dense stands of Pacific silver fir, mountain hemlock, Douglas fir, white pine and western cedar, Lost Lake sits in a steep, glacier-scoured mountain valley. Formed by a lava dam, it is fed by marshy Inlet Creek and springs on the east and west sides of the lake. Its outflow is the Lake Branch of the Hood River.

The triangle-shaped lake is 3.37 miles around the perimeter and is completely encircled by hiking trails. Boats are available to rent from the resort. A handicap-accessible fishing dock and a public launch are located on the eastern shore. No motors are allowed on the lake.

Rainbow trout are the main catch, but brown trout and kokanee are present, as well as smaller numbers of cutthroat and brook trout. ODFW supports the fishery with over 17,000 rainbows a year, including brood stock fish and surplus steelhead. Several fish in excess of eight pounds are landed each year.

At its deepest, the lake is 167 feet deep, with an average depth of 100 feet. The best trout fishing can be found in the corners and along the banks at the transitions to deeper water.

The best fishing is early in summer. By the third week of July, trout are well fed with bugs. By mid-September, trout begin to feed opportunistically again.

Insect hatches bring big fish into the shallows. Fly-fishermen should be prepared for matching a hatch of carpenter ants in early July. Expect hatches of little black mayflies (Nos. 12-14) and Hexagenia mayflies (No. 6) from middle of July to the end of the month.

Spin-fishermen do well with worms, salmon eggs and jar bait. A slow-trolled frog-pattern Flatfish is another favorite.

There are two roads that lead to the lake. The most reliable is the one accessed from Highway 35. The other route leads in from Zig Zag on Lolo Pass Road. Snow can keep this road sealed till early summer. Call the resort for road conditions.

LOCATION: Multnomah County

BEST TROUT/KOKANEE GEAR-FISHING TECHNIQUES

best good slow	Jan	Feb	Mar	Apr	May	Jun	Jul	Aug	Sep	Oct	Nov	Dec
Rainbow				6,7	1,5,6	1,5,6	5,7	5,7	1,5	1,5		
Brown				4,8	4,8	4,8	4,8	4,8	4,8	4,8		
Kokanee				8	8	2,8	2,8	2,8	2,8			

1. Spinner and worm troll
2. Kokanee Wedding Ring spinner and corn troll
3. Downrigger lake trout troll
4. Casting Lures: Injured-minnow imitation; spoon; spinner
5. Sliding sinker and jar bait
6. Bobber and bait
7. Spinning-rod fly and bubble
8. Kokanee/trout jigging

BEST FLY-FISHING TECHNIQUES

best good slow	Jan	Feb	Mar	Apr	May	Jun	Jul	Aug	Sep	Oct	Nov	Dec
Rainbow				2	2,5	1,2,3	1,2,4	2,5,7	2,5	2,5		
Brown				2	2,5	2,3	2,4	2,7	2,7	2		
Kokanee				5	5	5,7	5,7	5,7	5,7			

1. Two-fly Chironomid and indicator rig
2. Weighted streamer retrieve/ intermediate line leech retrieve
3. Dragonfly/damselfly nymph retrieves
4. Dry-fly dead-drift to rising trout
5. Wind drifting/trolling
6. Dry- fly with dropper nymph/Chironomid
7. Countdown method for sinking fly line

SERVICES

CAMPING & PARKS
- **Lost Lake Resort & Campground,** Hood River, 97031, (541) 386-6366, www.lostlakeresort.org

ACCOMMODATIONS
- **Seven Oaks B&B,** Hood River, 97031, (541) 386-7622, www.sevenoaksbb.com
- **Mt. Hood B&B,** Parkdale, 97041, (541) 352-6858, www.mthoodbnb.com
- **Old Parkdale Inn,** Parkdale, 97041, (541) 352-5551, www.hoodriverlodging.com

TACKLE SHOPS/BOAT RENTALS
- **Lost Lake Resort Tackle & Boat Rental,** Hood River, 97031, (541) 386-6366, www.lostlakeresort.org
- **Gorge Fly Shop,** Hood River, 97031, (541) 386-6977, www.gorgeflyshop.com

VISITOR INFORMATION
- **Mt. Hood National Forest,** Government Camp, 97028, (503) 668-1700, www.fs.usda.gov/mthood
- **Hood River County Chamber of Commerce,** Hood River, 97031, (800) 366-3530, (541) 386-2000, www.hoodriver.org

NEAREST CITIES/TOWNS
Hood River, 97031; Parkdale, 97041

VITAL STATISTICS

Surface Acres	321 acres
GPS coordinates	N 45 29.817' W 121 49.162'
Elevation	3140 feet
Depth	167 feet

AMENITIES

Resorts	Yes
Launches	2
Speed Limit	No motors
Campgrounds	114 sites
Day–Use Area	Yes
Boat Rental	Yes

BEST FOR FISHING
June–October

OTHER FAMILY ACTIVITIES
- Mt. Hood Railroad (Hood River to Parkdale)
- Mt. Hood National Forest
- Columbia River Gorge
- Hood River Valley Harvest Fest
- Mt. Hood Scenic Byway
- Bonneville Dam
- Wildlife watching
- Berry picking
- Hunting
- Hiking
- Mountain biking
- Camping
- Picnicking
- Birding
- Boating

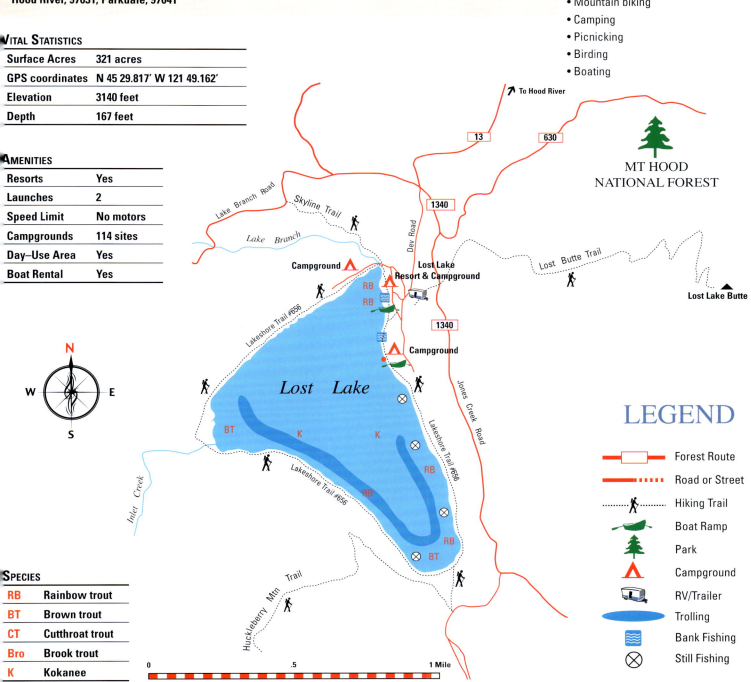

SPECIES

RB	Rainbow trout
BT	Brown trout
CT	Cutthroat trout
Bro	Brook trout
K	Kokanee

LEGEND

Forest Route	
Road or Street	
Hiking Trail	
Boat Ramp	
Park	
Campground	
RV/Trailer	
Trolling	
Bank Fishing	
Still Fishing	

Timothy Lake

Timothy Lake, 80 miles east of Portland, is a great place to wet a line in spring. The 1,282-acre reservoir in eastern Clackamas County gathers the waters of Crater Creek, Dinger Creek, Cooper Creek and the Oak Grove Fork of the Clackamas River to create a fantastic fishing resource for bank anglers and boaters.

The lake is famous for producing limits of kokanee and big brook trout. Brook trout grow fast, feeding on crayfish and snails. In June, the rainbow bite picks up, and it is possible to get holdover trout that range to 18 inches. Cutthroat trout are available as well. Fish the mouths of tributaries, smaller arms, and shallow water.

Until the lake warms up in summer, kokanee can be caught readily in the shallows on flies. For the best action, fish the mouths of tributaries, smaller arms, and shallow water.

When the water warms, the best kokanee fishing is in deeper water off the points and along the log boom near the dam. Some anglers set out a crayfish trap at the start of the day and eat their catch in the evening.

Bank fishermen set up at campgrounds and day-use areas, casting beyond the shallows to present their baits on the edge of deeper water. Trout are also caught in the 'no boat' zone by the dam and from a fantastic wheelchair-accessible T-shaped pier.

Boat launches, found at drive-in campgrounds, allow fishermen to reach water across the lake and present their lures and baits on seams along the northwest bank. When the water warms in summer, the best trout action is around the points and near tributary mouths.

LOCATION: Clackamas County

Photo by Gary Lewis

VITAL STATISTICS

Surface Acres	1282 acres
GPS coordinates	N 45 06.768' W 121 48.344'
Elevation	3217
Depth	80 feet

AMENITIES

Resorts	No
Launches	Six
Speed Limit	10 mph
Campgrounds	Five
Day-Use Area	Yes
Boat Rental	No

SPECIES

RB	**Rainbow trout**
CT	**Cutthroat trout**
Bro	**Brook trout**
K	**Kokanee**

Kokanee, brook trout, cutthroat and rainbows. This lake can provide fast action for big brooks early in the season and consistent limits of rainbows after the water warms in late spring.

BEST FLY-FISHING TECHNIQUES

best good slow	Jan	Feb	Mar	Apr	May	Jun	Jul	Aug	Sep	Oct	Nov	Dec
Rainbow				2	2,3,5	2,3,5	2,3,4,5	2,4,5	2,4,5	2		
Cutthroat				2	2,3,5	2,3,5	2,3,4,5	2,4,5	2,4,5	2		
Kokanee				5	5,6	5,6	5	5	5	2		
Brook				2	2,3,5	2,3,5	2,3,4,5	2,4,5	2,4,5	2		

1. Two-fly Chironomid and indicator rig
2. Weighted streamer retrieve/ intermediate line leech retrieve
3. Dragonfly/damselfly nymph retrieves
4. Dry-fly dead-drift to rising trout
5. Wind drifting/trolling
6. Dry-fly with dropper nymph/Chironomid
7. Countdown method for sinking fly line

BEST TROUT/KOKANEE GEAR-FISHING TECHNIQUES

best good slow	Jan	Feb	Mar	Apr	May	Jun	Jul	Aug	Sep	Oct	Nov	Dec
Rainbow				1	1,4	1,4,5	1,4,5	1,4,5	1,4,5	1,4,5		
Cutthroat				1	1,4	1,4,5	1,4,5	1,4,5	1,4,5	1,4,5		
Kokanee				8	8	2,8	2,8	2	2			
Brook				1,4,6	1,4,6	1,4,5	1,4,5	1,4,5	1,4,5	1,4,5		

1. Spinner and worm troll
2. Kokanee Wedding Ring spinner and corn troll
3. Downrigger lake trout troll
4. Casting Lures: Injured-minnow imitation; spoon; spinner
5. Sliding sinker and jar bait
6. Bobber and bait
7. Spinning-rod fly and bubble
8. Kokanee/trout jigging

BEST FOR FISHING

June–October

OTHER FAMILY ACTIVITIES

- USFS Museum nearby
- Hiking (13 miles around lake)
- Pacific Crest Trail runs along the northwest shore
- Birding
- Camping
- Picnicking

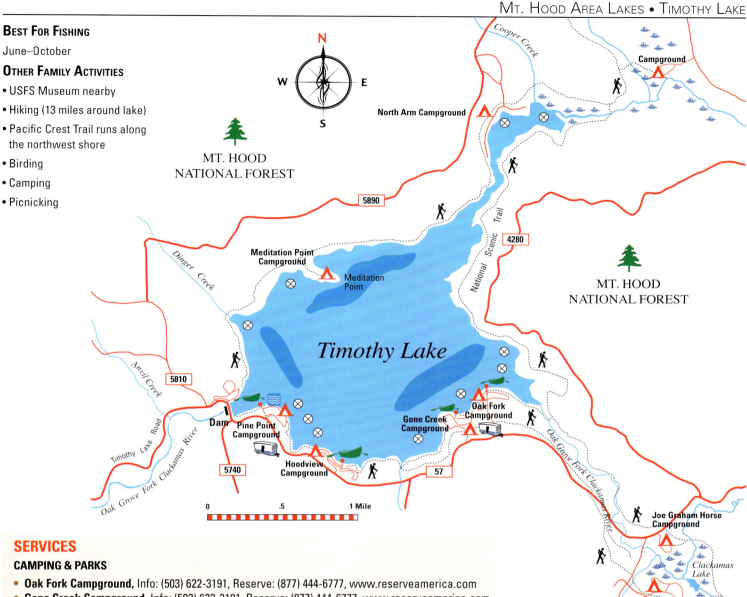

SERVICES

CAMPING & PARKS

- **Oak Fork Campground,** Info: (503) 622-3191, Reserve: (877) 444-6777, www.reserveamerica.com
- **Gone Creek Campground,** Info: (503) 622-3191, Reserve: (877) 444-6777, www.reserveamerica.com
- **Hoodview Campground,** Info: (503) 622-3191, Reserve: (877) 444-6777, www.reserveamerica.com
- **Pine Point Campground,** Info: (503) 622-3191, Reserve: (877) 444-6777, www.reserveamerica.com
- **Meditation Point Campground,** (503) 668-1700, hike-in or boat-in only, www.fs.usda.gov
- **North Arm Campground,** (503) 668-1700, www.fs.usda.gov
- **Joe Graham Horse Campground,** Info: (503) 622-3191, Reserve: (877) 444-6777, www.reserveamerica.com
- **Clackamas Lake Campground,** Info: (503) 622-3191, Reserve: (877) 444-6777, www.reserveamerica.com

ACCOMMODATIONS

- **Sandy Salmon B&B Lodge,** Sandy, 97055, (503) 622-6699, www.sandysalmon.com
- **Clackamas River House,** Oregon City, 97045, (503) 502-8478, www.clackamasriverhouse.com

TACKLE SHOPS/BOAT RENTALS

- **Dan-Dan Kitchen/Tailgate BBQ and Top Stop Chevron,** Government Camp, 97028, (503) 337-2277, www.DanDanKitchen.com
- **Estacada Tackle Shop,** Estacada, 97023, (503) 630-7424
- **The Fly Fishing Shop,** Welches, 97067, (800) 266-3971, (503) 622-4607, www.flyfishusa.com

VISITOR INFORMATION

- **Mt. Hood National Forest,** Government Camp, 97028, (503) 668-1700, www.fs.usda.gov/mthood
- **Estacada Chamber of Commerce,** Estacada, 97023, (503) 630-3483, www.estacadachamber.org
- **Mt. Hood Area Chamber of Commerce,** Welches, 97067, (503) 622-3017, www.mthoodchamber.com
- **Zigzag Ranger Station,** Zigzag, 97049, (503) 622-3191, www.fs.usda.gov

NEAREST CITIES/TOWNS

Government Camp, 97028; Estacada, 97023

LEGEND

━━━━━	Forest Route
━━ •••••	Road or Street
········ 🚶	Hiking Trail
🛶	Boat Ramp
🌲	Park
⛺	Campground
🚐	RV/Trailer
〰	Marsh or Swamp
⬭	Trolling
🌊	Bank Fishing
⊗	Still Fishing

Trillium Lake

On the slopes of Mount Hood, Trillium Lake is a favorite of many Portland-area fishermen. Rainbows in this pretty mountain lake average 8 to 14 inches. Cutthroat trout and brook trout are also found in Trillium. ODFW stocks this lake throughout the season with plenty of fish to keep anglers interested. Larger trout are planted in August and September. Fish that winter over can tip the scales at 3 pounds by next spring. With two launches, boat access is good. No motors are allowed.

Bank-bound fishermen find the best fishing on the south and eastern shores near the campground and day-use area. A handicapped-accessible fishing pier is very popular. Most anglers favor Power Bait, worms or salmon eggs. Rooster Tail spinners or small spoons tipped with bait can be very effective.

Bobbers keep baits out of the long grass. When fishing with jar baits, use a four- or five-foot leader.

Fly-fishermen can catch trout from the bank, but the best bet is to take to the water in a float tube or small boat. In the absence of surface activity, wind drift with a slow-sink fly line and a tandem rig or use an indicator and Chironomid setup.

For the biggest fish, hit Trillium when the snow melts and again at the end of the season. This lake is well-loved, especially in late June and early July. By September it is nearly forgotten, except by those who know that the fishing can be very good in fall.

LOCATION: Clackamas County

SERVICES

CAMPING & PARKS
- **Trillium Lake Campground,** (877) 444-6777, www.recreation.gov

ACCOMMODATIONS
- **Sandy Salmon B&B Lodge,** Sandy, 97055, (503) 622-6699, www.sandysalmon.com
- **Mt. Hood B&B,** Parkdale, 97041, (541) 352-6858, www.mthoodbnb.com
- **Old Parkdale Inn,** Parkdale, 97041, 541) 352-5551, hoodriverlodging.com
- **Doublegate Inn B&B,** Welches, 97067, (503) 622-0629, www.doublegateinn.com

TACKLE SHOPS/BOAT RENTALS
- **Dan-Dan Kitchen and Top Stop Chevron,** Government Camp, 97028, (503) 337-2277, www.DanDanKitchen.com
- **The Fly Fishing Shop,** Welches, 97067, (800) 266-3971, (503) 622-4607, www.flyfishusa.com

VISITOR INFORMATION
- **Mt. Hood National Forest,** Government Camp, 97028, (503) 668-1700, www.fs.usda.gov/mthood
- **Mt. Hood Area Chamber of Commerce,** Welches, 97067, (503) 622-3017, www.mthoodchamber.com
- **Zigzag Ranger Station,** Zigzag, 97049, (503) 622-3191, www.fs.usda.gov

NEAREST CITIES/TOWNS
Government Camp, 97028

Photo by Gary Lewis

In spring, Trillium is popular with Portland-area anglers. To sample this lake at its best, try it in the fall.

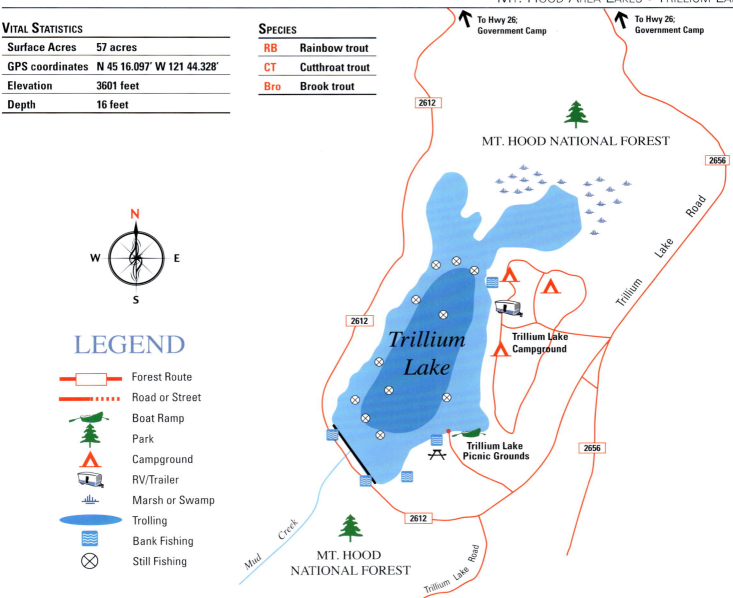

VITAL STATISTICS

Surface Acres	57 acres
GPS coordinates	N 45 16.097' W 121 44.328'
Elevation	3601 feet
Depth	16 feet

SPECIES

RB	Rainbow trout
CT	Cutthroat trout
Bro	Brook trout

LEGEND

	Forest Route
	Road or Street
	Boat Ramp
	Park
	Campground
	RV/Trailer
	Marsh or Swamp
	Trolling
	Bank Fishing
⊗	Still Fishing

BEST FLY-FISHING TECHNIQUES

best good slow	Jan	Feb	Mar	Apr	May	Jun	Jul	Aug	Sep	Oct	Nov	Dec
Rainbow				2	2,5	1,3,4,5	1,3,4,5	1,3,4,5	4,5	2,5		
Cutthroat				2	2,5	1,3,4,5	1,3,4,5	1,3,4,5	4,5	2,5		
Brook				2	2,5	1,3,4,5	1,3,4,5	1,3,4,5	4,5	2,5		

1. Two-fly Chironomid and indicator rig
2. Weighted streamer retrieve/intermediate line leech retrieve
3. Dragonfly/damselfly nymph retrieves
4. Dry-fly dead-drift to rising trout
5. Wind drifting/trolling
6. Dry-fly with dropper nymph/Chironomid
7. Countdown method for sinking fly line

BEST TROUT/KOKANEE GEAR-FISHING TECHNIQUES

best good slow	Jan	Feb	Mar	Apr	May	Jun	Jul	Aug	Sep	Oct	Nov	Dec
Rainbow				5,6	5,6	1,5,6,7	1,5,6,7	1,5,7	1,5,7	5,7		
Cutthroat				5,6	5,6	1,5,6,7	1,5,6,7	1,5,7	1,5,7	5,7		
Brook				5,6	5,6	1,5,6,7	1,5,6,7	1,5,7	1,5,7	5,7		

1. Spinner and worm troll
2. Kokanee Wedding Ring spinner and corn troll
3. Downrigger lake trout troll
4. Casting Lures: Injured-minnow imitation; spoon; spinner
5. Sliding sinker and jar bait
6. Bobber and bait
7. Spinning-rod fly and bubble
8. Kokanee/trout jigging

AMENITIES

Resorts	No
Launches	Two
Speed Limit	No motors
Campgrounds	Yes
Day-Use Area	Yes
Boat Rental	No

BEST FOR FISHING

May–October

OTHER FAMILY ACTIVITIES

• Birding
• Camping
• Picnicking
• Hiking

Lake Billy Chinook

Some reservoirs obliterate the landscape, leaving little trace of the history and geology beneath the surface. But at Lake Billy Chinook, it's not hard to imagine the old river channels—the Deschutes, Crooked and Metolius and their confluence, now obscured by 4,000 surface acres and up to 415 feet of water.

Round Butte Dam was finished in 1965 and the power of the water harnessed by three 1000-kilowatt generators. Today, the entire Pelton Round Butte complex generates enough energy to power a city the size of Salem.

In Lake Billy Chinook (a.k.a. Round Butte Reservoir), bull trout run 18 inches to 10 pounds or more. Every year, fish in the low teens are caught. Oregon's state–record bull trout came out of this lake in 1989, a fish that tipped the scales at over 23 pounds.

In spring, bull trout chase kokanee and smallmouth bass throughout the reservoir. When water temperatures go above 55°F, the bull trout follow the kokes deeper. In spring, rig with 12-pound test and cast large minnow imitations in the transition zones between the shallows and deeper water. Start with an 8-inch imitation. There are times when smaller baits work, but the big bulls don't get that way by being picky.

Restrictive catch regulations have ensured a thriving bull trout population. You may find them in all arms of the lake, but if you fish the Metolius channel you'll need a Warm Springs Reservation fishing permit. This can be purchased in the nearby town of Culver on the way to the water.

Most anglers use hard baits, but swim baits are also a good choice. An erratic retrieve drives the bull trout wild. A few anglers fly-fish for bull trout.

This is finesse fishing that's appropriate whenever you find a bull trout feeding on fish they've chased into shoreside cover. Your casts need not be pretty, but they must reach well away from the boat. Cast, let the fly sink, then start to bring it back with long, erratic strips, punctuated by long pauses. The pause will often bring the strike as the bull trout sees its prey stop and turn slightly, hackles flaring in the sudden loss of tension.

Kokanee angling is popular here and anglers turn to the landlocked sockeye salmon in May, reaching them with jigs early in the season. Trolling often pays off better later in the year. Rainbows and brown trout are caught most often closer to running water in the mouths of the Deschutes, Crooked River or Metolius.

A lot of anglers are unaware of the smallmouth bass that live in the shoreside structure. In summer and fall, they can be tempted by a plastic worm or Rooster Tail spinner.

Lake Billy Chinook is one of the most popular reservoirs in Central Oregon. In summer months, plan on sharing the water with powerboats and jet-skis.

LOCATION: Jefferson County

VITAL STATISTICS

Surface Acres	3916
GPS coordinates	N 44 36.09' W 121 16.52'
Elevation	1945 feet
Depth	415 feet

AMENITIES

Resorts	Yes
Launches	6
Speed Limit	No
Campgrounds	3
Day-Use Area	Yes
Boat Rental	Yes

SPECIES

K	Kokanee
Bul	Bull trout
RB	Rainbow trout
BT	Brown trout
SB	Smallmouth bass

Photo by Gary Lewis

Brett Dennis admires a nice bull trout from Lake Billy Chinook. A new fish-passage facility is changing the dynamic of this popular fishing reservoir, making it possible for runs of sockeye, steelhead and salmon to reach the ocean and return to their native streams.

BEST TROUT/KOKANEE GEAR-FISHING TECHNIQUES

best good slow	Jan	Feb	Mar	Apr	May	Jun	Jul	Aug	Sep	Oct	Nov	Dec
Bull Trout			4	4	4	3,8	3,8	3,8	3,4,8	4		
Kokanee			8	8	8	2,8	2,8	2	2	2		
Rainbow			4	4	4	4	4	4	4	4		
Brown			4	4	4,8	4,8	4,8	4,8	4,8	4		

1. Spinner and worm troll
2. Kokanee Wedding Ring spinner and corn troll
3. Downrigger lake trout troll
4. Casting Lures: Injured-minnow imitation; spoon; spinner
5. Sliding sinker and jar bait
6. Bobber and bait
7. Spinning-rod fly and bubble
8. Kokanee/trout jigging

BEST FOR FISHING
March–October

OTHER FAMILY ACTIVITIES
• Birding
• Camping
• Boating

SERVICES

CAMPING & PARKS

- **Lake Billy Chinook Houseboats,** Redmond, 97756, (877) 546-7171, (541) 504-5951, www.lakebillychinook.com
- **Three Rivers Marina,** Culver, 97734, (541) 233-8743, www.threerm.com
- **The Cove Palisades State Park,** Info: (800) 551-6949, Reserve: (800) 452-5687, www.oregonstateparks.org
- **Redmond/Central Oregon KOA,** Culver, 97734, Reserve: (800) 562-1992 Info: (541) 546-3046, www.koa.com/campgrounds/redmond

ACCOMMODATIONS

- **Cove Palisades Resort & Marina** (houseboat rentals), Culver, 97734, (877) 546-7171, (541) 546-9999, www.covepalisadesresort.com
- **Sweet Virginia's B&B,** Metolius, 97741, (541) 546-3031, www.sweetvirginiasbedandbreakfast.com
- **Eagle Crest Resort,** Redmond, 97756, (800) 682-4786, (855) 682-4786, www.eagle-crest.com

TACKLE SHOPS/BOAT RENTALS

- **Cove Palisades Resort & Marina,** Culver, 97734, (541) 546-9999, www.covepalisadesresort.com
- **Brad's Bait & Tackle,** Madras, 97741, (541) 475-6892, www.bradsbaitandtackle.com
- **Camp Sherman Store,** Camp Sherman, 97730, (541) 595-6711, www.campshermanstore.com
- **Fin and Fire,** Redmond, 97756, (541) 548-1503, (866)-275-2810, www.finandfire.com
- **Bi-Mart,** Madras, 97741, (541) 475-1394, www.bimart.com
- **Central Oregon Stillwater Outfitters,** Sunriver, 97707, (541) 598-0008, www.centraloregonfishing.com
- **Rick's Trophy Mounts** (taxidermy), (541) 480-1570, www.trophytroutguide.com

VISITOR INFORMATION

- **Crooked River National Grassland,** Madras, 97741, (541) 475-9272, www.fs.usda.gov
- **Madras-Jefferson County Chamber of Commerce,** Madras, 97741, (541) 475-2350, www.madraschamber.com
- **The Confederated Tribes of Warm Springs,** Warm Springs, 97761, (541) 553-1161, www.warmsprings.com
- **Fishing Central Oregon,** www.fishingcentraloregon.com

NEAREST CITIES/TOWNS

Madras, 97741; Culver, 97734

BEST FLY-FISHING TECHNIQUES

best	good	slow	Jan	Feb	Mar	Apr	May	Jun	Jul	Aug	Sep	Oct	Nov	Dec
Bull Trout					2	2	2	7	7	7	2	2		
Kokanee					7	7	7	7	7	7	7	7		
Rainbow					2	2	2	2	2	2	2	2		
Brown					2	2	2	2	2	2	2	2		

1. Two-fly Chironomid and indicator rig
2. Weighted streamer retrieve/ intermediate line leech retrieve
3. Dragonfly/damselfly nymph retrieves
4. Dry-fly dead-drift to rising trout
5. Wind drifting/trolling
6. Dry-fly with dropper nymph/Chironomid
7. Countdown method for sinking fly line

BEST BASS AND PANFISH TECHNIQUES

best	good	slow	Jan	Feb	Mar	Apr	May	Jun	Jul	Aug	Sep	Oct	Nov	Dec
Smallmouth						3	3	3,7	3,7	3,7	3,7	3		

1. Carolina rig
2. Spinner bait
3. Crappie jig
4. Dropshot
5. Crankbait
6. Top-water plug/ buzzbait
7. Senko worm rig

LEGEND

- ▭ Forest Route
- ▬ Road or Street
- ⛵ Boat Ramp
- 🌲 Park
- ⛺ Campground
- 🚐 RV/Trailer

0   .5   1 Mile

Crane Prairie Reservoir

A trip to Crane Prairie is unlike any other fishing experience in Oregon. Its size, fluctuation and composition make it a complex fishery and its habitat provides diverse wildlife-viewing opportunities.

Cultus, Deschutes and Quinn rivers empty into the lake and their old channels still carve its bottom. The trees that lined the riverbanks still stand, mute testimony to the dam that was built in 1928, forming the reservoir.

Mergansers and mallards, cormorants and coots paddle among the standing trees. Canada geese wheel against the sky.

Crane Prairie fell on hard times with the illegal introduction of largemouth bass, crappie and stickleback. The bass and crappie eat the smaller trout and the two-inch stickleback compete for the insects. To improve fishing, Department of Fish and Wildlife has been releasing larger trout, the effort has paid off.

When the water is high, trout are scattered throughout the lake. As the level comes down though, trout will be found in the deepest water. The trick is finding the old river channels. As the average lake temperature warms, the fish move into the cooler river channels and use them as highways to move around. The channels average 12 to 13 feet deep and are relatively weed-free with a sandy or silty floor.

Power Bait, worms and dragonfly nymphs are the standbys for the reservoir's still-fishermen.

Fly-rodders imitate damsel and dragonfly nymphs, stickleback minnows, mayflies and Chironomids (midge larvae). Chironomids are midges, which look a little like mosquitoes, but lack the bite. On Crane Prairie, midges make up close to 40 percent of a trout's annual food intake. Since they are used to

Doug Sanders caught this 13 ½-pound Crane Prairie rainbow on a gray beadhead Hare's Ear.
Photo by Gary Lewis

eating Chironomids year-round, trout are vulnerable to a well-presented pattern at any time.

It may not be the most exciting form of fly-fishing, but fishing these small patterns under water is one of the most effective techniques you can learn. This is because most of what a trout eats, it finds under water.

There are two stages of the Chironomid's life that are most important to fly-fishermen. The larval stage can be imitated by bloodworm patterns. Red, maroon, brown, black, purple, and olive are good choices. The pupal phase is where the insect is most vulnerable. The Bronzie, sized No. 12-14, is a good pattern to imitate this stage.

Use a floating line. Tie on a 15-foot leader and position the strike indicator to suspend the fly about one or more feet above the vegetation. In this stage, the pupa sheds the larval shuck and wiggles from the bottom to the surface, rising slowly at a 90-degree angle.

Cast and let the line drift with the wind, keeping the line straight and paying close attention to the indicator. Wave action on the water will make your imitation appear to wiggle.

In spring, bass, bluegill and crappie are found in the shallows where the water is warmest. Plastic worms account for many of the bass taken. Trout-pattern crankbaits work very well.

Crane Prairie's bass are fish-eaters. Don't be afraid to use large baits, such as deep-diving crankbaits or minnow imitations. Probe the deepest water near fish-holding structure like submerged timber or rocky points.

Bank anglers can catch fish at Crane Prairie, outcroppings of lava rock and forest limit shoreline access. The best fishing is from a boat.

BEST TROUT/KOKANEE GEAR-FISHING TECHNIQUES

best good slow	Jan	Feb	Mar	Apr	May	Jun	Jul	Aug	Sep	Oct	Nov	Dec
Rainbow				1,5,7	5,6,7	5,6,7	5,6,7	5,6,7	5,6,7	5,6,7		
Brook				1,5,7	5,6,7	5,6,7	5,6,7	5,6,7	5,6,7	5,6,7		

1. Spinner and worm troll
2. Kokanee Wedding Ring spinner and corn troll
3. Downrigger lake trout troll
4. Casting Lures: Injured-minnow imitation; spoon; spinner
5. Sliding sinker and jar bait
6. Bobber and bait
7. Spinning-rod fly and bubble
8. Kokanee/trout jigging

AMENITIES

Resorts	Crane Prairie Resort
Launches	6
Speed Limit	10mph
Campgrounds	Developed and primitive
Day-Use Area	Yes
Boat Rental	Crane Prairie Resort

BEST FLY-FISHING TECHNIQUES

best good slow	Jan	Feb	Mar	Apr	May	Jun	Jul	Aug	Sep	Oct	Nov	Dec
Rainbow				1,2	1,2	1	1	1	1	1,2		
Brook				2	2	2	2	2	2	2		

1. Two-fly Chironomid and indicator rig
2. Weighted streamer retrieve/intermediate line leech retrieve
3. Dragonfly/damselfly nymph retrieves
4. Dry-fly dead-drift to rising trout
5. Wind drifting/trolling
6. Dry-fly with dropper nymph/Chironomid
7. Countdown method for sinking fly line

SPECIES

RB	Rainbow trout
Bro	Brook trout
K	Kokanee
LB	Largemouth bass

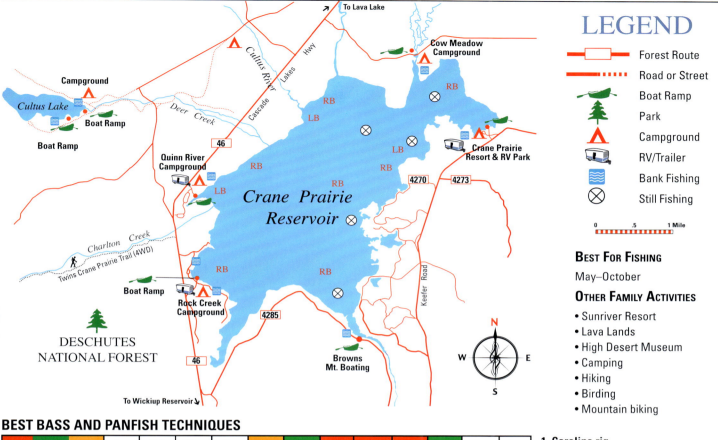

LEGEND

	Forest Route
	Road or Street
	Boat Ramp
	Park
	Campground
	RV/Trailer
	Bank Fishing
	Still Fishing

0 .5 1 Mile

BEST FOR FISHING
May–October

OTHER FAMILY ACTIVITIES
- Sunriver Resort
- Lava Lands
- High Desert Museum
- Camping
- Hiking
- Birding
- Mountain biking

BEST BASS AND PANFISH TECHNIQUES

best	good	slow	Jan	Feb	Mar	Apr	May	Jun	Jul	Aug	Sep	Oct	Nov	Dec
Largemouth							1	1,5	5,6	4,6,7	1,2,7	1,2,7		

VITAL STATISTICS

Surface Acres	varies up to 4960
GPS coordinates	N 43 47.937' W 121 45.497'
Elevation	4445 feet
Depth	20 feet

LOCATION: Deschutes County

1. Carolina rig
2. Spinner bait
3. Crappie jig
4. Dropshot
5. Crankbait
6. Top-water plug/buzzbait
7. Senko worm rig

SERVICES

CAMPING & PARKS
- **Crane Prairie Resort & RV Park**, Bend, 97709, (541) 383-3939, www.crane-prairie-resort-guides.com
- **Cow Meadow Campground**, (541) 383-5300, www.fs.usda.gov
- **Quinn River Campground**, Reserve: (877) 444-6777, www.fs.usda.gov
- **Rock Creek Campground**, Info: (541) 383-5300, www.fs.usda.gov

ACCOMMODATIONS
- **The Mill Inn B&B**, Bend, 97701, (541) 389-9198, (877) 748-1200, www.millinn.com
- **Lara House Bed and Breakfast**, Bend, 97701, (800) 766-4064, (541) 388-4064, www.larahouse.com
- **Juniper Acres B&B**, Bend, 97701, (541) 389-2193, www.juniperacres.com

TACKLE SHOPS/BOAT RENTALS
- **The Patient Angler Fly Shop**, Bend, 97702, (541) 389-6208, www.patientangler.com
- **Confluence Fly Shop**, Bend, 97702, (541) 678-5633, www.confluenceflyshop.com
- **Wholesale Sports Outdoor Outfitters**, Bend, 97701, (541) 693-5000, (800) 696-0253, www.ca.wholesalesports.com
- **Mickey Finn Guides**, Bend, 97709, (541) 383-3939, www.crane-prairie-resort-guides.com

- **Central Oregon Stillwater Outfitters**, Sunriver, 97707, (541) 598-0008, www.centraloregonfishing.com
- **Fly & Field Outfitters**, Bend, 97702, (866) 800-2812, (541) 318-1616, www.flyandfield.com
- **Sunriver Fly Shop**, Sunriver, 97707, (541) 593-8814, www.sunriverflyshop.com
- **The Hook Fly Shop**, Sunriver, 97707, (888) 230-4665, (541) 593-2358, www.hookfish.com
- **Rick's Trophy Mounts** (taxidermy), (541) 480-1570, www.trophytroutguide.com

VISITOR INFORMATION
- **Willamette National Forest**, (541) 225-6300, www.fs.usda.gov/willamette
- **Deschutes National Forest**, Bend, 97701, (541) 383-5300, www.fs.usda.gov/centraloregon
- **Bend Chamber of Commerce**, Bend, 97701, (541) 382-3221, www.bendchamber.org
- **Sunriver Area Chamber of Commerce**, Sunriver, 97707, (541) 593-8149, www.sunriverchamber.com
- **Central Oregon Visitors Association**, Bend, 97702, (800) 800-8334, www.visitcentraloregon.com
- **Fishing Central Oregon**, www.fishingcentraloregon.com

NEAREST CITIES/TOWNS
Sunriver, 97707; Bend, 97701

Davis Lake
Fly-Fishing Only

Named for 'Button' Davis, a 19th century cattleman, Davis Lake is one of the largest lakes on the central Cascade slope. Fed by Odell Creek, Ranger Creek and Moore Creek, the lake is drained through several sumps in the lava. Surrounded by lava flows, forests of ponderosa pine and meadows, this lake is one of the jewels of central Oregon.

Davis is a barbless-hooks-fly-fishing-only lake with a reputation for turning out big rainbows. But what was once a trophy-trout fishery, has become a big-bass factory. Illegally introduced largemouth are on the ascendancy.

The productive water is rich with insects, including dragonflies and damselflies, leeches and tui chub. Chironomids are abundant early in the season. *Callibaetis* mayflies are a major trout food source in May and June.

Early in the season, trout and bass seek the warm shallows. The cool waters found at the creek inlets offer the best place to catch a rainbow in the summer.

When targeting trout, long fluorocarbon leaders and intermediate sinking lines come into play in a big way.

Largemouth prowl the edges of the tules and along the lava flow but you may find bass anywhere in the lake. For bass, use an 8-weight rod and big cork poppers or six-inch Bunny Leech patterns. Anglers are encouraged to keep the bass. There is no limit for bass.

Four boat launches provide access to the water. Often, during July and August, the lake is too low to launch a boat. Bring a car-top pram or canoe and be prepared to walk it to the water.

Gary Lewis shows off a Davis Lake bass that fell for a purple Bunny Leech. Big Bunny Leeches and crayfish patterns work best when the bass are deep at midday. During morning and evening, surface flies are a good choice.

AMENITIES

Resorts	No
Launches	4
Speed Limit	10
Campgrounds	Yes
Day-Use Area	Yes
Boat Rental	No

VITAL STATISTICS

Surface Acres	3906
GPS coordinates	N 43 36.04' W 121 49.41'
Elevation	4386 feet
Depth	20 feet

SPECIES

LB	Largemouth bass
RB	Rainbow trout

SERVICES

CAMPING & PARKS

- **Lava Flow North Campground,** (541) 383-5300, www.fs.usda.gov
- **East Davis Lake Campground,** (541) 383-5300, www.fs.usda.gov
- **Willamette National Forest,** (541) 225-6300, www.fs.usda.gov/willamette
- **Deschutes National Forest,** Bend, 97701, (541) 383-5300, www.fs.usda.gov/centraloregon

ACCOMMODATIONS

- **The Mill Inn B&B,** Bend, 97701, (541) 389-9198, (877) 748-1200, www.millinn.com
- **Lara House B&B,** Bend, 97701, (541) 388-4064, www.larahouse.com
- **Juniper Acres B&B,** Bend, 97701, (541) 389-2193, www.juniperacres.com

TACKLE SHOPS/BOAT RENTALS

- **The Patient Angler Fly Shop,** Bend, 97702, (541) 389-6208, www.patientangler.com
- **Confluence Fly Shop,** Bend, 97702, (541) 678-5633, www.confluenceflyshop.com
- **Wholesale Sports Outdoor Outfitters,** Bend, 97701, (541) 693-5000, (800) 696-0253, www.ca.wholesalesports.com
- **Mickey Finn Guides,** Bend, 97709, (541) 383-3939, www.crane-prairie-resort-guides.com

- **Central Oregon Stillwater Outfitters,** Sunriver, 97707, (541) 598-0008, www.centraloregonfishing.com
- **Fly & Field Outfitters,** Bend, 97702, (866) 800-2812, (541) 318-1616, www.flyandfield.com
- **Sunriver Fly Shop,** Sunriver, 97707, (541) 593-8814, www.sunriverflyshop.com
- **The Hook Fly Shop,** Sunriver, 97707, (888) 230-4665, (541) 593-2358, www.hookfish.com

VISITOR INFORMATION

- **Bend Chamber of Commerce,** Bend, 97701, (541) 382-3221, www.bendchamber.org
- **Sunriver Area Chamber of Commerce,** Sunriver, 97707, (541) 593-8149, www.sunriverchamber.com
- **La Pine Chamber of Commerce,** La Pine, 97739, (541) 536-9771, www.lapine.org
- **Central Oregon Visitors Association,** Bend, 97702, (800) 800-8334, www.visitcentraloregon.com
- **Fishing Central Oregon,** www.fishingcentraloregon.com

NEAREST CITIES/TOWNS

Crescent, 97733; La Pine, 97739; Sunriver, 97707; Bend, 97701

BEST FOR FISHING

May–October

OTHER FAMILY ACTIVITIES

- Sunriver Resort
- Lava Lands
- High Desert Museum
- Camping
- Hiking
- Birding
- Mountain biking

LOCATION: Deschutes & Klamath Counties

BEST FLY-FISHING TECHNIQUES

1. Two-fly Chironomid and indicator rig
2. Weighted streamer retrieve/intermediate line leech retrieve
3. Dragonfly/damselfly nymph retrieves
4. Dry-fly dead-drift to rising trout
5. Wind drifting/trolling
6. Dry-fly with dropper nymph/Chironomid
7. Countdown method for sinking fly line

best	good	slow	Jan	Feb	Mar	Apr	May	Jun	Jul	Aug	Sep	Oct	Nov	Dec
Rainbow							1,2,3	1,3,5	1,3,5	1	1,3,5	1,2,5		
Largemouth							2	2	2	2	2	2		

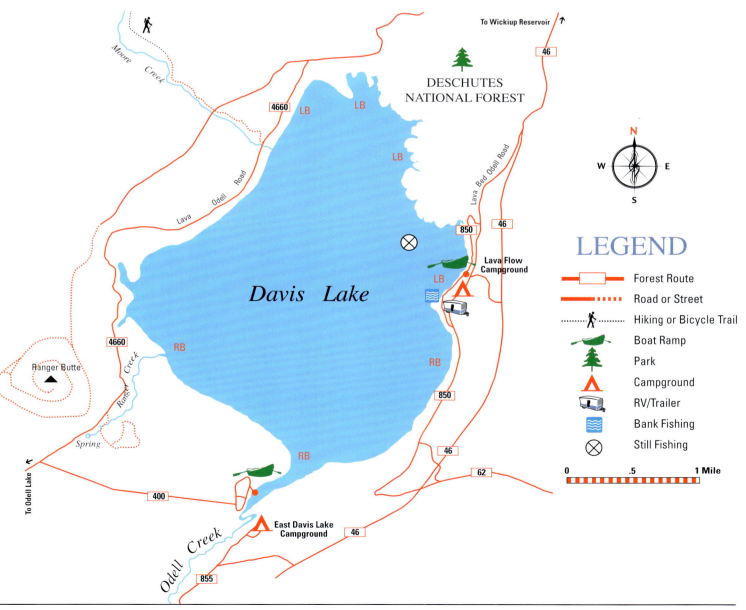

East Lake / Paulina Lake

Scott Cook shows off a typical East Lake rainbow. One popular pursuit on this lake is the quest for the East Lake Slam — a rainbow, brown trout, kokanee and Atlantic salmon.

Photo by Gary Lewis

East Lake and Paulina Lake have long been famous for trophy brown trout. Paulina currently holds the state record and it is generally believed that when the record falls again, it will be a fish from Paulina that replaces it. In both waters, brown trout catches range between 12 and 18 inches, but it's not uncommon to tangle with a trout in the 7- to 10-pound range.

East Lake is one of the most productive lakes in the state. Rainbow trout fishing peaks in July with reliable hatches of mayflies and midges. Leeches and baitfish are other important foods. Brown, black and olive streamers can imitate damselflies and dragonflies, as well as leeches and minnows depending upon the retrieve.

Browns can be caught shallow in the early morning and late evening. They are found around steep drop-offs and rock shelves in deeper water.

Atlantic salmon average 10 to 15 inches and are often caught by fly rodders plying the edges of the weedbeds on East Lake's eastern shore.

Kokanee, which average 12 to 17 inches, are found in both lakes. Jigging works best early in the season and trolling takes more trout later in the season. Fly-anglers can take kokanee all season long on wind-drifted Callibaetis nymphs.

Casting lures from a boat to the shore in early spring and in fall is an effective method for catching large brown trout and rainbows. Try a brown Rooster Tail when the sun is low in the sky. Trolling or casting for big brown trout with minnow-imitating crankbaits brings success.

When temperatures drop in the fall, fish move into shallow water to feed. Fish at this time of year become irritable and strike out of aggression. Target weedbeds, rock slides and downed timber, but don't overlook areas with gravel bottoms or underwater springs.

There is a $10 Monument entry fee that applies to each vehicle unless the destination is East Lake Resort or Paulina Lake Lodge.

LOCATION: Deschutes County

EAST LAKE SPECIES

RB	Rainbow trout
BT	Brown trout
K	Kokanee
AS	Atlantic salmon

PAULINA LAKE SPECIES

RB	Rainbow trout
BT	Brown trout
K	Kokanee

BEST TROUT/KOKANEE GEAR-FISHING TECHNIQUES

best good slow	Jan	Feb	Mar	Apr	May	Jun	Jul	Aug	Sep	Oct	Nov	Dec
Rainbow				4,5	4,5	1,5,7	1,5,7	1,5,7	1,5,7	1,5,7		
Brown				4	4,8	4,8	4,8	4,8	4,8	4,8		
Atlantic Salmon				7	7	1,7	1,7	1,7	1,7	1,7		
Kokanee				8	8	2,8	2,8	2	2	2		

1. Spinner and worm troll
2. Kokanee Wedding Ring spinner and corn troll
3. Downrigger lake trout troll
4. Casting Lures: Injured-minnow imitation; spoon; spinner
5. Sliding sinker and jar bait
6. Bobber and bait
7. Spinning-rod fly and bubble
8. Kokanee/trout jigging

BEST FLY-FISHING TECHNIQUES

best good slow	Jan	Feb	Mar	Apr	May	Jun	Jul	Aug	Sep	Oct	Nov	Dec
Rainbow				2	2,5	1,2,3,5	3,4,5,7	3,4,5,7	3,4,5,7	1,2,5,7		
Brown				2	2,5	1,2,3,5	3,4,5,7	3,4,5,7	3,4,5,7	1,2,5,7		
Atlantic Salmon				2	2,5	1,2,3,5	3,4,5,7	3,4,5,7	3,4,5,7	1,2,5,7		
Kokanee				5	5	3,5,7	3,5,7	3,5,7	3,5,7	2		

1. Two-fly Chironomid and indicator rig
2. Weighted streamer retrieve/intermediate line leech retrieve
3. Dragonfly/damselfly nymph retrieves
4. Dry-fly dead-drift to rising trout
5. Wind drifting/trolling
6. Dry-fly with dropper nymph/Chironomid
7. Countdown method for sinking fly line

BEST FOR FISHING

May–October

OTHER FAMILY ACTIVITIES

• Newberry National Volcanic Monument
• Sunriver Resort
• Paulina Plunge Bike Trail
• Paulina Falls Trail
• Paulina Peak
• Obsidian Flow hike
• Hot Springs
• Lava Lands
• High Desert Museum
• Camping

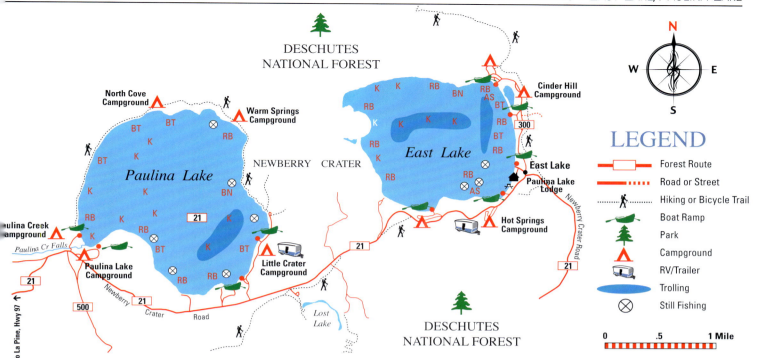

AMENITIES	
Resorts	2
Launches	At campgrounds and day-use areas
Speed Limit	10 mph
Campgrounds	7
Day-Use Area	Yes
Boat Rental	Yes

PAULINA LAKE VITAL STATISTICS	
Surface Acres	1531
GPS coordinates	N 43 42.47' W 121 16.26'
Elevation	6331 feet
Depth	250 feet

EAST LAKE VITAL STATISTICS	
Surface Acres	1044
GPS coordinates	N 43 43.04' W 121 12.53'
Elevation	6370 feet
Depth	180 feet

SERVICES

CAMPING & PARKS

- **East Lake Resort**, La Pine, 97739, (541) 536-2230, www.eastlakeresort.com
- **Cinder Hill Campground**, (877) 444-6777, www.reserveamerica.com
- **East Lake Campground**, (541) 383-5300, www.fs.usda.gov
- **Little Crater Campground**, (541) 383-5300, www.fs.usda.gov
- **Paulina Lake Campground**, (877) 444-6777, www.reserveamerica.com
- **North Cove Campground**, hike-in only, www.hikercentral.com/campgrounds/117802.html
- **Warm Springs Campground**, hike-in only, www.hikercentral.com/campgrounds/117852.html
- **Paulina Lake Lodge**, La Pine, 97739, (541) 536-2230, www.paulinalakelodge.com

ACCOMMODATIONS

- **The Mill Inn B&B**, Bend, 97701, (541) 389-9198, (877) 748-1200, www.millinn.com
- **Lara House B&B**, Bend, 97701, (541) 388-4064, www.larahouse.com
- **Juniper Acres B&B**, Bend, 97701, (541) 389-2193, www.juniperacres.com

TACKLE SHOPS/BOAT RENTALS

- **The Patient Angler Fly Shop**, Bend, 97702, (541) 389-6208, www.patientangler.com
- **Confluence Fly Shop**, Bend, 97702, (541) 678-5633, www.confluenceflyshop.com
- **Wholesale Sports Outdoor Outfitters**, Bend, 97701, (541) 693-5000, (800) 696-0253, www.ca.wholesalesports.com

- **Mickey Finn Guides**, Bend, 97709, (541) 383-3939, www.crane-prairie-resort-guides.com
- **Central Oregon Stillwater Outfitters**, Sunriver, 97707, (541) 598-0008, www.centraloregonfishing.com
- **Fly & Field Outfitters**, Bend, 97702, (866) 800-2812, (541) 318-1616, www.flyandfield.com
- **Sunriver Fly Shop**, Sunriver, 97707, (541) 593-8814, www.sunriverflyshop.com
- **The Hook Fly Shop**, Sunriver, 97707, (888) 230-4665, (541) 593-2358, www.hookfish.com

VISITOR INFORMATION

- **Newberry National Volcanic Monument**, Info: (541) 383-5700, www.fs.usda.gov
- **Lava Lands Visitor Center**, Bend, 97707, (541) 593-2421, www.fs.usda.gov
- **Central Oregon Visitors Association**, Bend, 97702, (800) 800-8334, www.visitcentraloregon.com
- **Deschutes National Forest**, Bend, 97701, (541) 383-5300, www.fs.usda.gov/centraloregon
- **Bend Chamber of Commerce**, Bend, 97701, (541) 382-3221, www.bendchamber.org
- **Sunriver Area Chamber of Commerce**, Sunriver, 97707, (541) 593-8149, www.sunriverchamber.com
- **Atlas of Oregon Lakes**, www.aol.research.pdx.edu
- **Fishing Central Oregon**, www.fishingcentraloregon.com

NEAREST CITIES/TOWNS

Sunriver, 97707; Bend, 97701; La Pine, 97739

Gold Lake

Photo by Gary Lewis

David Miller probes the depths of Gold Lake for rainbows and brook trout.

Gold Lake is a food-rich mountain still water fed by Salt Creek, its waters filtered through a swamp. Rainbows are the main quarry, but small brook trout can provide fast action.

Located high in the Willamette National Forest, Gold Lake is a 96-acre oval surrounded by Engelmann spruce, subalpine fir and mountain hemlock. It is a trout lake with the right combination of shallow water and depths to foster good insect growth and protection in cold winters. Rainbows are stocked in the summer and brook trout are prolific.

Fishing is limited to fly-fishing only and no motors are allowed on the lake. Gold Lake is fed by Salt Creek, filtered through a sphagnum swamp and springs at the north corner. At the southwest end, Salt Creek flows out of the lake. The tributary is closed to fishing.

The water has good clarity, but organic matter drained through the bog, is suspended in the column, which gives a brownish tint. With the evening sun on the lake, the water takes on a golden hue.

The bogs and shallows are host to rich insect life. Fly-anglers should be prepared to match hatches of Callibaetis and other mayflies, caddis, damselflies, dragonflies, midges and mosquitoes. If the wind comes up, ants may be blown onto the surface. As with most mountain lakes, limit fly selection to smaller sizes: Nos. 12-16 for dry flies; Nos. 10-14 for nymphs and soft-hackle wet flies; Nos. 8-10 for streamers and leeches.

Anglers typically bring more brook trout to the net. Here, the brookies average 6 to 10 inches, while the rainbows run 10 to 14 inches. There is no limit on the number of brook trout an angler can keep.

Gold Lake is well-loved, but there is room for anglers to spread out. Canoes, kayaks, pontoon boats and float tubes are perfect watercraft for the lake. The campground is suited to small RVs and tent campers, with pit toilets and picnic tables. Hiking trails provide access along the shore. Bring mosquito repellent.

The adjacent 463-acre subalpine sphagnum swamp, named the Gold Lake Bog Research National Area, contains rare vegetation. Formal permission from the U.S. Forest Service, is required to visit the bog.

LOCATION: Lane County

BEST FLY-FISHING TECHNIQUES

best	good	slow	Jan	Feb	Mar	Apr	May	Jun	Jul	Aug	Sep	Oct	Nov	Dec
Rainbow							2,3	1,2,3	1,2,3,4	1,2,4,5	1,2,4,5	1,2,5		
Brook							2,3	2,3,5	2,3,5	2,5	2,5	2,5		

1. **Two-fly Chironomid and indicator rig**
2. **Weighted streamer retrieve/intermediate line leech retrieve**
3. **Dragonfly/damselfly nymph retrieves**
4. **Dry-fly dead-drift to rising trout**
5. **Wind drifting/trolling**
6. **Dry-fly with dropper nymph/Chironomid**
7. **Countdown method for sinking fly line**

BEST FOR FISHING

June–October

OTHER FAMILY ACTIVITIES

• Salt Creek Falls
• Diamond Peak Hike
• Westfir Covered Bridge
• Huckleberry picking
• Birding
• Camping

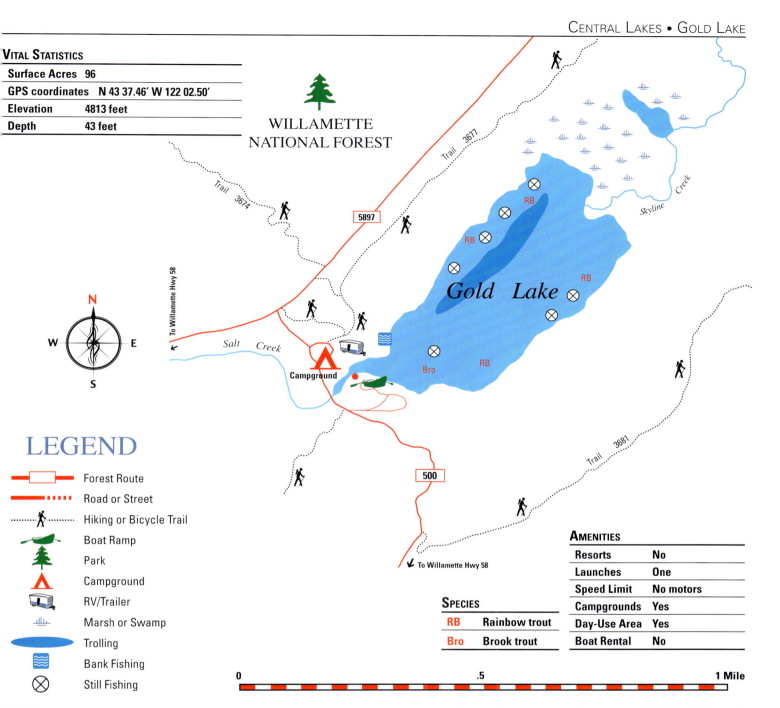

VITAL STATISTICS

Surface Acres	96
GPS coordinates	N 43 37.46' W 122 02.50'
Elevation	4813 feet
Depth	43 feet

WILLAMETTE
NATIONAL FOREST

LEGEND

	Forest Route
	Road or Street
	Hiking or Bicycle Trail
	Boat Ramp
	Park
	Campground
	RV/Trailer
	Marsh or Swamp
	Trolling
	Bank Fishing
	Still Fishing

SPECIES

RB	Rainbow trout
Bro	Brook trout

AMENITIES

Resorts	No
Launches	One
Speed Limit	No motors
Campgrounds	Yes
Day-Use Area	Yes
Boat Rental	No

0 .5 1 Mile

SERVICES

CAMPING & PARKS

- **Gold Lake Campground**, Westfir, 97492, info: Middle Fork Ranger Station, (541) 782-2283, www.fs.usda.gov
- **Big Pines RV Park**, Crescent, 97733, (541) 433-2785, www.bigpinesrvpark.com
- **Crescent Lake Resort**, Crescent, 97733, (541) 433-2505, www.crescentlakeresort.com
- **Crescent Junction RV**, Crescent, 97733, (541) 433-5300, www.crescentjunctionrv.com

ACCOMMODATIONS

- **Oakridge Lodge & Guest House**, Oakridge, 97463, (541) 782-4000, www.oakridge-lodge.com
- **Odell Lake Lodge & Resort**, Crescent, 97733, (541) 433-2540, www.odelllakeresort.com
- **Shelter Cove Resort & Marina**, Cascade Summit, 97733, outside Oregon: (800) 647-2729, (541) 433-2548, www.sheltercoveresort.com

TACKLE SHOPS/BOAT RENTALS

- **Ken's Sporting Goods**, Crescent, 97733, (541) 433-2530, www.kenssportinggoods-or.com
- **Bert-Fish-N-Stuff**, Oakridge, 97463, (541) 782-2136
- **Odell Sportsman Center**, Crescent Lake, 97733, (541) 433-9355

VISITOR INFORMATION

- **Willamette National Forest**, www.fs.usda.gov/willamette
- **Central Oregon Visitors Association**, Bend, 97702, (800) 800-8334, www.visitcentraloregon.com
- **North Klamath County**, www.NorthKlamathCounty.org
- **City of Oakridge**, Oakridge, 97463, (541) 782-2258, www.ci.oakridge.or.us
- **Oakridge-Westfir Chamber of Commerce**, Oakridge, 97463, (541) 782-4146, www.2chambers.com
- **Fishing Central Oregon**, www.fishingcentraloregon.com

NEAREST CITIES/TOWNS

Crescent, 97733; Oakridge, 97463

Hosmer Lake

O ne of central Oregon's best-loved waters is a little jewel called Hosmer Lake. Reflected mountaintops ripple in the glassy water. Wind whispers in the pines and an osprey plunges from its lofty perch to grasp a fish in its talons. Fly-rodders fish from float tubes, pontoon boats, and canoes, trying to tempt trout with feathered morsels. Bait of any kind is not found on Hosmer, nor are gas engines.

Brook trout and Atlantic salmon are what draw the fishermen and keep the osprey interested. Hosmer is one of only two places in the state where a fisherman can catch an Atlantic salmon.

Once known by the humble handle of Mud Lake, for the murky water stirred by the tails of carp and other trash fish, the lake was killed with rotenone in 1957. A new name was applied in honor of Paul Hosmer, a long-time resident of Bend.

Formed by volcanic activity, lava outcroppings add character to the shore. Marshes and moss extend into the lake; the bottom is composed of mud and peat.

Atlantic salmon have been in the lake since 1958 and brook trout are plentiful. Fishing at Hosmer is limited to barbless hooks, fly-angling only.

Be prepared to match hatches of *Callibaetis* and other mayflies, caddis, damselflies, dragonflies and midges. If the wind comes up, ants may be blown onto the water.

Atlantic salmon and brook trout average 10 to 12 inches, but brook trout to six pounds can be glimpsed in the narrows. Plan to fish until dark and go small. That

Known for its idyllic setting and big-fish potential, Hosmer Lake attracts fly-fishermen from all over the state to do battle with Atlantic salmon, rainbows and brook trout.

means using long leaders, 7X tippets and No. 20 Callibaetis emergers, micro caddis or midges. Bring a flashlight, it can be hard to tie tiny flies with wispy tippets, not to mention how badly your hands shake when fish are rising all around.

SERVICES

CAMPING & PARKS

- **Deschutes National Forest,** Bend, 97701, (541) 383-5300, www.fs.usda.gov/centraloregon
- **Willamette National Forest,** (541) 225-6300, www.fs.usda.gov/willamette
- **South Campground,** (541) 383-5300, www.fs.usda.gov
- **Mallard Marsh Campground,** (541) 383-5300, www.fs.usda.gov
- **Elk Lake Campground,** (541) 383-5300, www.fs.usda.gov
- **Point Campground,** (541) 383-5300, www.fs.usda.gov
- **Little Fawn,** Reserve: (877) 444-6777, (541) 383-5300, www.fs.usda.gov
- **Elk Lodge Resort,** Bend, 97701, (541) 480-7378, www.elklakeresort.net

ACCOMMODATIONS

- **The Mill Inn B&B,** Bend, 97701, (541) 389-9198, (877) 748-1200, www.millinn.com
- **Lara House B&B,** Bend, 97701, (800) 766-4064, (541) 388-4064, www.larahouse.com
- **Juniper Acres B&B,** Bend, 97701, (541) 389-2193, www.juniperacres.com

TACKLE SHOPS/BOAT RENTALS

- **The Patient Angler Fly Shop,** Bend, 97702, (541) 389-6208, www.patientangler.com
- **Confluence Fly Shop,** Bend, 97702, (541) 678-5633, www.confluenceflyshop.com
- **Wholesale Sports Outdoor Outfitters,** Bend, 97701, (541) 693-5000, (800) 696-0253, www.ca.wholesalesports.com

- **Mickey Finn Guides,** Bend, 97709, (541) 383-3939, www.crane-prairie-resort-guides.com
- **Central Oregon Stillwater Outfitters,** Sunriver, 97707, (541) 598-0008, www.centraloregonfishing.com
- **Fly & Field Outfitters,** Bend, 97702, (866) 800-2812, (541) 318-1616, www.flyandfield.com
- **Sunriver Fly Shop,** Sunriver, 97707, (541) 593-8814, www.sunriverflyshop.com
- **The Hook Fly Shop,** Sunriver, 97707, (888) 230-4665, (541) 593-2358, www.hookfish.com

VISITOR INFORMATION

- **Bend Chamber of Commerce,** Bend, 97701, (541) 382-3221, www.bendchamber.org
- **Sunriver Area Chamber of Commerce,** Sunriver, 97707, (541) 593-8149, www.sunriverchamber.com
- **Central Oregon Visitors Association,** Bend, 97702, (800) 800-8334, www.visitcentraloregon.com
- **Outdoor Project,** Info for camping, boating, hiking, etc., www.outdoorproject.com
- **Fishing Central Oregon,** www.fishingcentraloregon.com

NEAREST CITIES/TOWNS

Sunriver, 97707; Bend, 97701

BEST FLY-FISHING TECHNIQUES

best	good	slow	Jan	Feb	Mar	Apr	May	Jun	Jul	Aug	Sep	Oct	Nov	Dec
Rainbow							1,2,4	1,2,4,5	1,2,4,5	1,4,6	1,4,6	1,4,6		
Brook							2,3	2,3	2,5	2,5	2,5	2,5		
Atlantic Salmon							1,2,4	1,2,4,5	1,2,4,5	1,4,6	1,4,6	1,4,6		

1. Two-fly Chironomid and indicator rig
2. Weighted streamer retrieve/intermediate line leech retrieve
3. Dragonfly/damselfly nymph retrieves
4. Dry-fly dead-drift to rising trout
5. Wind drifting/trolling
6. Dry-fly with dropper nymph/Chironomid
7. Countdown method for sinking fly line

AMENITIES

Resorts	No
Launches	1
Speed Limit	No motors
Campgrounds	Yes
Day-Use Area	Yes
Boat Rental	No

SPECIES

RB	Rainbow trout
AS	Atlantic salmon
Bro	Brook trout

VITAL STATISTICS

Surface Acres	198
GPS coordinates	N 43 57.21' W 121 47.01'
Elevation	4966 feet
Depth	12 feet

BEST FOR FISHING

June–October

OTHER FAMILY ACTIVITIES

- Elk Lake Resort
- Mt. Bachelor
- Hiking
- Camping
- Picnicking
- Birding
- Kayaking

LOCATION: Deschutes County

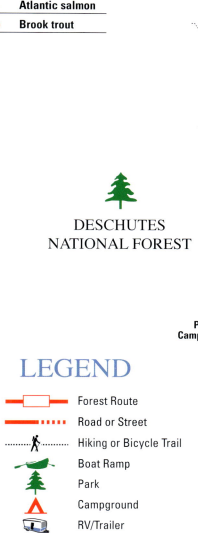

LEGEND

▭	Forest Route
▬▬	Road or Street
·····𝕩····	Hiking or Bicycle Trail
🛶	Boat Ramp
🌲	Park
🔺	Campground
🚐	RV/Trailer
≈	Marsh or Swamp
▨	Bank Fishing

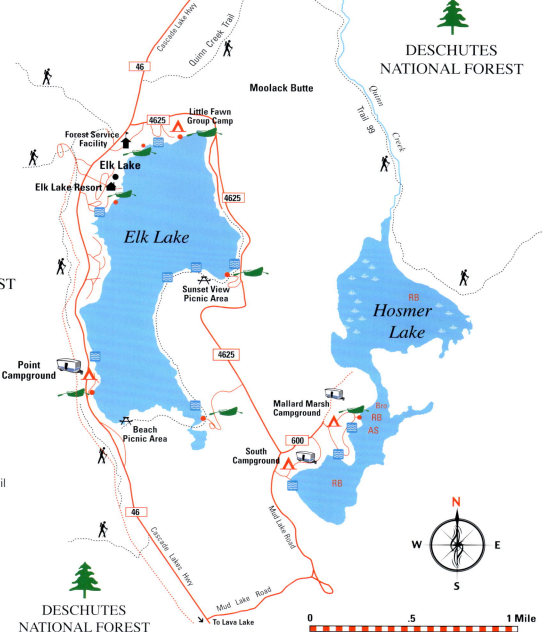

Lava Lake

Photo by Gary Lewis

One of the most productive still waters in the state, Lava Lake is capable of turning out limits of big rainbows throughout the season.

Fed by springs and marshes and bounded by lava outcrops and pine forest, Lava Lake is a scenic spot and one of the most productive fishing waters in Central Oregon. Mt. Bachelor, South Sister and Broken Top are visible from the shoreline. It is a good place to bring the family for a boat ride and a great place to net a limit of big, fat rainbows.

Trout grow fast here. On years when the lake is accessible on Opening Day, anglers can catch fish from the bank by casting lures or employing jar baits. By June and July, the trout average 15 inches; 18-inch rainbows are not uncommon in a five-fish limit.

ODFW stocks rainbows as six-inchers. The typical rainbow more than doubles in size by the next season. The key to Lava's fishing is its insect life. Shallow waters and weeds promote abundant insects and fish gorge themselves during the season.

Most anglers use a boat here. A hiking trail takes off from the campground and runs along the east side of the lake. Velveeta Point, on the eastern shore, is one of the best bank fishing spots. Another is near the public launch. Trolling pays off early in the season, running a circuit close to the eastern shore and returning through the middle of the lake. Fly-anglers do well when they ply the waters along the western bank. Still-fishermen anchor or drift near Velveeta Point and along the east side.

The lake is easy to read. Outcroppings, marshes, shoals and rushes break up the shoreline. The average depth is 20 feet. Water level fluctuates with snow melt. Weed growth in the summer can limit trolling efforts. The fish are still there, but they are easier caught with still-fishing techniques.

Nearby, Little Lava Lake is another good place to hook into a rainbow, brook or brown. If you plan a trip to Lava Lake between June and August, bring mosquito juice or a head net.

SERVICES

CAMPING & PARKS

- **Deschutes National Forest,** Bend, 97701, (541) 383-5300, www.fs.usda.gov/centraloregon
- **Lava Lake Campground,** www.fs.usda.gov
- **Little Lava Lake Campground,** Reserve: (877) 444-6777, Info: (541) 383-5300, www.fs.usda.gov
- **Lava Lake Lodge,** (541) 383-5300, www.fs.usda.gov

ACCOMMODATIONS

- **The Mill Inn B&B,** Bend, 97701, (541) 389-9198, (877) 748-1200, www.millinn.com
- **Lara House B&B,** Bend, 97701, (541) 388-4064, www.larahouse.com
- **Juniper Acres B&B,** Bend, 97701, (541) 389-2193, www.juniperacres.com

TACKLE SHOPS/BOAT RENTALS

- **The Patient Angler Fly Shop,** Bend, 97702, (541) 389-6208, www.patientangler.com
- **Confluence Fly Shop,** Bend, 97702, (541) 678-5633, www.confluenceflyshop.com
- **Wholesale Sports Outdoor Outfitters,** Bend, 97701, (541) 693-5000, (800) 696-0253, www.ca.wholesalesports.com
- **Mickey Finn Guides,** Bend, 97709, (541) 383-3939, www.crane-prairie-resort-guides.com

- **Central Oregon Stillwater Outfitters,** Sunriver, 97707, (541) 598-0008, www.centraloregonfishing.com
- **Fly & Field Outfitters,** Bend, 97702, (866) 800-2812, (541) 318-1616, www.flyandfield.com
- **Sunriver Fly Shop,** Sunriver, 97707, (541) 593-8814, www.sunriverflyshop.com
- **The Hook Fly Shop,** Sunriver, 97707, (888) 230-4665, (541) 593-2358, www.hookfish.com

VISITOR INFORMATION

- **Bend Chamber of Commerce,** Bend, 97701, (541) 382-3221, www.bendchamber.org
- **Sunriver Area Chamber of Commerce,** Sunriver, 97707, (541) 593-8149, www.sunriverchamber.com
- **Central Oregon Visitors Association,** Bend, 97702, (800) 800-8334, www.visitcentraloregon.com
- **Lava Lands Visitor Center,** Bend, 97707, (541) 593-2421, www.fs.usda.gov
- **Outdoor Project,** Info for camping, boating, hiking, etc., www.outdoorproject.com
- **Fishing Central Oregon,** www.fishingcentraloregon.com

NEAREST CITIES/TOWNS

Sunriver, 97707; Bend, 97701

LOCATION: Deschutes County

BEST FOR FISHING

April–October

OTHER FAMILY ACTIVITIES

- Sunriver Resort
- Camping
- Wildlife watching
- Hiking
- Picnicking

SPECIES

RB	Rainbow trout
Bro	Brook trout

BEST TROUT/KOKANEE GEAR-FISHING TECHNIQUES

best	good	slow	Jan	Feb	Mar	Apr	May	Jun	Jul	Aug	Sep	Oct	Nov	Dec
Rainbow						1,4,5,7	1,4,5,7	5,7	5,7	5,7	5,7	1,4,5,7		
Brook						5,7	5,7	5,7	5,7	5,7	5,7	5,7		

1. Spinner and worm troll
2. Kokanee Wedding Ring spinner and corn troll
3. Downrigger lake trout troll
4. Casting Lures: Injured-minnow imitation; spoon; spinner
5. Sliding sinker and jar bait
6. Bobber and bait
7. Spinning- rod fly and bubble
8. Kokanee/trout jigging

BEST FLY-FISHING TECHNIQUES

best	good	slow	Jan	Feb	Mar	Apr	May	Jun	Jul	Aug	Sep	Oct	Nov	Dec
Rainbow						2,7	2,7	1,3,5,7	1,4,5,7	1,4,5,7	1,2,5,7	1,2,5,7		
Brook						2,7	2,7	1,3,5,7	1,4,5,7	1,4,5,7	1,2,5,7	1,2,5,7		

1. Two-fly Chironomid and indicator rig
2. Weighted streamer retrieve/intermediate line leech retrieve
3. Dragonfly/damselfly nymph retrieves
4. Dry-fly dead-drift to rising trout
5. Wind drifting/trolling
6. Dry-fly with dropper nymph/Chironomid
7. Countdown method for sinking fly line

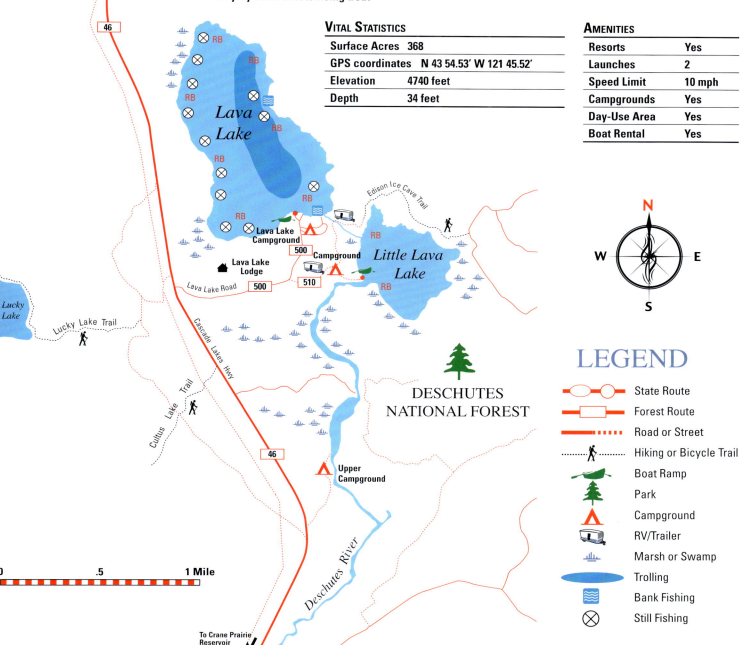

VITAL STATISTICS

Surface Acres	368
GPS coordinates	N 43 54.53' W 121 45.52'
Elevation	4740 feet
Depth	34 feet

AMENITIES

Resorts	Yes
Launches	2
Speed Limit	10 mph
Campgrounds	Yes
Day-Use Area	Yes
Boat Rental	Yes

LEGEND

- State Route
- Forest Route
- Road or Street
- Hiking or Bicycle Trail
- Boat Ramp
- Park
- Campground
- RV/Trailer
- Marsh or Swamp
- Trolling
- Bank Fishing
- Still Fishing

Odell Lake

It's hard to find a pairing that goes better together than a Big Mac and a large Coke. But for my money, I'll take my big macks and large kokes from a Cascade lake.

Odell Lake (and nearby Crescent) are some of the coldest, deepest lakes in the state, which makes them good habitat for a big char we call lake trout or mackinaw. Odell and Crescent also have good populations of kokanee (a landlocked sockeye salmon), the lake trout's favorite food.

Lake trout and kokanee aren't native to Odell Lake, but they've been there since the 1950s, long enough for a lake trout from Odell to set the state record at over 40 pounds. So far this year, Odell Lake's biggest fish tipped the scales at 33 pounds.

The lake trout move up and down in the water column on a daily basis. Find the right depth on the fishfinder then troll a Hoochie or large Flatfish or Kwikfish behind a series of flashers. Bait with a large trailing nightcrawler to add scent. Ring the dinner bell by dropping the downrigger into the mud, then cranking it back up again.

At Odell you can target one in the morning and the other in the afternoon. If you've been targeting macks, you've likely found the kokanee already.

Kokanee feed in schools of similar-sized fish and can be easy to catch when conditions are right. Full-grown, they average 12 to 18 inches. As soon as the sun hits the water, the plankton go deeper and kokanee follow. Like their nemesis, kokanee are most easily enticed in early morning, but they can be invited to dinner at lunchtime as well.

Gary Lewis with an Odell Lake mackinaw. Big lake trout feed heavily on kokanee. Find the kokanee and you often find lake trout feeding or resting nearby.

Jigging is a favorite technique early in the year, but trollers seem to do better in summer. An easy rig, whether using a downrigger or not, consists of an eight-inch flasher on the main line with four feet of leader terminated at an Apex or Wedding Ring spinner. Most anglers add white corn and season it by adding a scent like Pautzke's Krill.

Sometimes you have to look beyond the easier-caught small fry and try for a fish that takes two hands to hold on to. When you want to catch a trophy, troll deep and order up a big mack. For all-day action, go for kokes.

LOCATION: Klamath County

BEST TROUT/KOKANEE GEAR-FISHING TECHNIQUES

best	good	slow	Jan	Feb	Mar	Apr	May	Jun	Jul	Aug	Sep	Oct	Nov	Dec
Lake Trout						4	3,4	3	3	3	3	3,4,8		
Rainbow						1,4,8	1,4,8	1,4,8	1,4,8	1,4,8	1,4,8	1,4,8		
Kokanee						8	8	2,8	2,8	2	2			

1. Spinner and worm troll
2. Kokanee Wedding Ring spinner and corn troll
3. Downrigger lake trout troll
4. Casting Lures: Injured-minnow imitation; spoon; spinner
5. Sliding sinker and jar bait
6. Bobber and bait
7. Spinning-rod fly and bubble
8. Kokanee/trout jigging

BEST FLY-FISHING TECHNIQUES

best	good	slow	Jan	Feb	Mar	Apr	May	Jun	Jul	Aug	Sep	Oct	Nov	Dec
Lake Trout						2	2,7	2,7	2,7	2,7	2,7	2		
Rainbow						2	2	2,3,4	2,3,4	2,3,4	2,3	2,3		
Kokanee						5	5	5	5	5	5			

1. Two-fly Chironomid and indicator rig
2. Weighted streamer retrieve/intermediate line leech retrieve
3. Dragonfly/damselfly nymph retrieves
4. Dry-fly dead-drift to rising trout
5. Wind drifting/trolling
6. Dry-fly with dropper nymph/Chironomid
7. Countdown method for sinking fly line

SPECIES

K	Kokanee
RB	Rainbow trout
LT	Lake trout
W	Whitefish
Bul	Bull trout (protected)

BEST FOR FISHING

May–October

OTHER FAMILY ACTIVITIES

- Salt Creek Falls
- Diamond Peak Hike
- Westfir Covered Bridge
- Huckleberry picking
- Birding
- Hunting
- Camping

SERVICES

CAMPING & PARKS

- **Deschutes National Forest**, Bend, 97701, (541) 383-5300, www.fs.usda.gov/centraloregon
- **Odell Lake Lodge & Resort**, Crescent, 97733, (541) 433-2540, www.odelllakeresort.com
- **Shelter Cove Resort & Marina**, Cascade Summit, 97733 (541) 433-2548, outside Oregon: (800) 647-2729, www.sheltercoveresort.com
- **Princess Creek Campground**, (541) 383-5300, www.fs.usda.gov
- **Sunset Cove Campground**, (541) 383-5300, www.fs.usda.gov
- **Trapper Creek Campground**, Reserve: (877) 444-6777, Info: (541) 338-7869, www.recreation.gov
- **Crescent Lake Resort**, Crescent, 97733, (541) 433-2505, www.crescentlakeresort.com
- **Crescent Junction RV**, Crescent, 97733, (541) 433-5300, www.crescentjunctionrv.com

ACCOMMODATIONS

- **Oakridge Lodge & Guest House**, Oakridge, 97463, (541) 782-4000, www.oakridge-lodge.com
- **Odell Lake Lodge & Resort**, Crescent, 97733, (541) 433-2540, www.odelllakeresort.com

- **Shelter Cove Resort & Marina**, Cascade Summit, 97733, (541) 433-2548, outside Oregon: (800) 647-2729, www.sheltercoveresort.com

TACKLE SHOPS/BOAT RENTALS

- **Ken's Sporting Goods**, Crescent, 97733, (541) 433-2530, www.kenssportinggoods-or.com
- **Bert-Fish-N-Stuff**, Oakridge, 97463, (541) 782-2136
- **Odell Sportsman Center**, Crescent Lake, 97733, (541) 433-9355
- **L&M Catchin'**, Stanfield, 97875, (541) 433-2548, (guide)

VISITOR INFORMATION

- **Central Oregon Visitors Association**, Bend, 97702, (800) 800-8334, www.visitcentraloregon.com
- **North Klamath County**, www.NorthKlamathCounty.org
- **City of Oakridge**, Oakridge, 97463, (541) 782-2258, www.ci.oakridge.or.us
- **Oakridge-Westfir Chamber of Commerce**, Oakridge, 97463, (541) 782-4146, www.2chambers.com

NEAREST CITIES/TOWNS
Crescent, 97733; Oakridge, 97463

AMENITIES

Resorts	2
Launches	5
Campgrounds	Yes
Day-Use Area	Yes

VITAL STATISTICS

Surface Acres	3582
GPS coordinates	N 43 32.932' W 121 57.773'
Elevation	4787 feet
Depth	282 feet

DESCHUTES NATIONAL FOREST

LEGEND

State Route	
Forest Route	
Road or Street	
Hiking or Bicycle Trail	
Boat Ramp	
Park	
Campground	
RV/Trailer	
Marsh or Swamp	
Trolling	
Bank Fishing	
Still Fishing	

To Oakridge

58

Gold Lake Sno Park

North Rosary Lake

Middle Rosary Lake

Lower Rosary Lake

58

Pacific Crest National Scenic Trail

Burley Bluff

Princess Cr

Princess Creek Campground

Trapper Creek Campground

Shelter Cove Resort & Marina

West Bay Cr

Shelter Cove

Kok

Breezy Point

Pebble Bay

Odell Lake

Salmon Creek

Little Cr

Quita Cr

Douglas Cr

Antler Cr

58

0   .5   1 Mile

Crystal Creek

Roosevelt Point

Serenity Bay

Trapper Creek

Wharf Creek

Sunset Cove Campground

Chiquapin Point

680

Odell Creek

Crater Butte Pacific Trail

Odell Lake Lodge & Resort

Odell Lake

58

To Hwy 97

N
W   E
S

Prineville Reservoir

Photo by Gary Lewis

Prineville Reservoir covers 3,000 surface acres at full pool. A popular place for water-skiers in the summertime, this long narrow impoundment can produce fast action for crappie, bass and trout.

Prineville Reservoir is a large impoundment, located 15 miles southeast of Prineville, formed by a dam on Crooked River. Created mainly for flood control and irrigation, the reservoir fluctuates in size. Many different species are found in the lake.

The lake is planted with fingerling rainbows in May of each year. By the end of their first winter, these fish average 12 to 14 inches with some running to 17 inches. Prineville Reservoir is productive trout water that also supports populations of smallmouth bass, largemouth, crappie and catfish. The reservoir is deep in places, but there is a lot of shallow water along the banks. Good insect production and a healthy crayfish population help trout and bass grow fast.

Look at the topography of the shoreline for an indication where to concentrate your efforts. Rocky points or steep shoulders give indication that a ridge continues below the surface. This type of structure will hold feeding rainbows in the morning and evening.

Good bank fishing can be found in Powder House Cove, near Bowman Dam and in Prineville Reservoir State Park up to Jasper Point.

A favorite trout bait is the Prineville Sandwich. One variation employs a No. 8 red bait hook with a Pautzke's single egg, a green, garlic-flavored marshmallow and a bit of nightcrawler. Trout can't resist it, but the bite is a tricky one. Wait until the rod tip has bounced a few times and the line starts to move.

Trolling is an effective way to take rainbows. Use a flasher with a nightcrawler behind it, or troll a lone spinner like the black and green Panther Martin. Concentrate on the shallows and edge cover, along drop-offs. Troll along the cliffs opposite the resort and around the islands and points.

The lake is loaded with crappie. They average six to seven inches, but bigger fish are available. Crappie can be found throughout the lake. Use a red, yellow or chartreuse jig, tipped with a bit of bait. Best bets are near shoreside structure like riprap and cliff walls. Keep every one you catch—for the table or for the garden—there is no limit.

Good trout fishing can be found year-round in Crooked River, for eight miles downstream from Bowman Dam. Check regulations.

LOCATION: Crook County

BEST FOR FISHING

April–October

OTHER FAMILY ACTIVITIES

- Boating
- Waterskiing
- Camping
- Hunting
- Hiking
- Birding
- Museum

SPECIES

RB	Rainbow trout
CT	Cutthroat trout
LB	Largemouth bass
SB	Smallmouth bass
Cr	Crappie
BC	Bullhead catfish

SERVICES

CAMPING & PARKS

- **Ochoco National Forest,** Prineville, 97754, (541) 416-6500, www.fs.usda.gov
- **Deschutes National Forest,** Bend, 97701, (541) 383-5300, www.fs.usda.gov/centraloregon
- **Jasper Point,** Info: (800) 551-6949, Park: (541) 447-4363, www.oregonstateparks.org
- **Prineville Reservoir State Park,** Reserve: (800) 452-5687, (541) 447-4363, www.reserveamerica.com
- **Prineville Reservoir Resort,** Prineville, 97754, (541) 447-7468, www.prinevillereservoirresort.com

ACCOMMODATIONS

- **Bellavista B&B,** Prineville, 97754 (541) 416-2400, www.bellavistab-b.com
- **Lara House B&B,** Bend, 97701, (541) 388-4064, www.larahouse.com
- **Juniper Acres B&B,** Bend, 97701, (541) 389-2193, www.juniperacres.com
- **The Mill Inn B&B,** Bend, 97701, (541) 389-9198, (877) 748-1200, www.millinn.com

TACKLE SHOPS/BOAT RENTALS

- **Prineville Reservoir Resort,** Prineville, 97754, (541) 447-7468, www.prinevillereservoirresort.com
- **Patrick's Cent Wise Sporting Goods,** Redmond, 97756, (541) 548-2334
- **Prepper Up,** Prineville, 97754, (541) 447-6930, www.prepperup.com
- **L&M Catchin',** Stanfield, 97875, (541) 433-2548, (guide)

VISITOR INFORMATION

- **Central Oregon Visitors Association,** Bend, 97702, (800) 800-8334, www.visitcentraloregon.com
- **Bend Chamber of Commerce,** Bend, 97701, (541) 382-3221, www.bendchamber.org
- **Prineville-Crook County Chamber,** Prineville, 97754, (541) 447-6304, www.visitprineville.org
- **Atlas of Oregon Lakes,** www.aol.research.pdx.edu
- **Fishing Central Oregon,** www.fishingcentraloregon.com

NEAREST CITIES/TOWNS

Prineville, 97754; Bend, 97701

BEST TROUT/KOKANEE GEAR-FISHING TECHNIQUES

best	good	slow	Jan	Feb	Mar	Apr	May	Jun	Jul	Aug	Sep	Oct	Nov	Dec
Rainbow			1,5	1,5	1,5	1,4,5	1,4,5	1,4,5	1,4,5	1,4,5	1,4,5	1,4,5	1,5	1,5

1. Spinner and worm troll
2. Kokanee Wedding Ring spinner and corn troll
3. Downrigger lake trout troll
4. Casting Lures: Injured minnow imitation; spoon; spinner
5. Sliding sinker and jar bait
6. Bobber and bait
7. Spinning-rod fly and bubble
8. Kokanee/trout jigging

BEST FLY-FISHING TECHNIQUES

best	good	slow	Jan	Feb	Mar	Apr	May	Jun	Jul	Aug	Sep	Oct	Nov	Dec
Rainbow			2	2	2	1,2	1,2	1,2	1,2	1,2	1,2	2	2	2

1. Two-fly Chironomid and indicator rig
2. Weighted streamer retrieve/intermediate line leech retrieve
3. Dragonfly/damselfly nymph retrieves
4. Dry-fly dead-drift to rising trout
5. Wind drifting/trolling
6. Dry fly with dropper nymph/Chironomid
7. Countdown method for sinking fly line

BEST BASS AND PANFISH TECHNIQUES

best	good	slow	Jan	Feb	Mar	Apr	May	Jun	Jul	Aug	Sep	Oct	Nov	Dec
Largemouth						1,4,7	1,4,7	1,4,7	2,5,6	2,5,6	2,5	4,7		
Smallmouth						3,4	3,5	3,5	3,5,7	3,5,7	3,5,7	3,4		
Crappie						3	3	3	3	3	3	3		

1. Carolina rig
2. Spinner bait
3. Crappie jig
4. Dropshot
5. Crankbait
6. Top-water plug/buzzbait
7. Senko worm rig

VITAL STATISTICS

Surface Acres	3136
GPS coordinates	N 44 06.38' W 120 47.07'
Elevation	3235 feet
Depth	130 feet

AMENITIES

Resorts	Yes
Launches	5
Speed Limit	No
Campgrounds	Yes
Day-Use Area	Yes
Boat Rental	Yes

LEGEND

 State Route
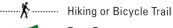 Road or Street
 Hiking or Bicycle Trail
Boat Ramp
Park
Campground
RV/Trailer
Bank Fishing

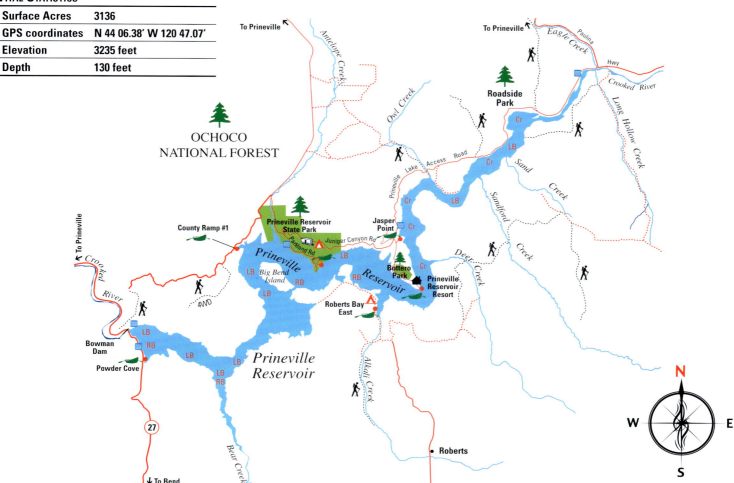

Wickiup Reservoir

Work started on Wickiup Reservoir in 1939, but World War II slowed construction. The dam was completed in 1949 and one of Oregon's most productive trout fisheries was born. This water-storage reservoir is one of the largest in the state and its waters harbor rainbows and brown trout of legendary proportion.

Fed by the Upper Deschutes via Crane Prairie, the Davis Lake sump, Davis Creek, Browns Creek and several springs, some of the best fishing is in the old channels. At its deepest, the lake is 70 feet deep, but average depth is 20 feet. A depth finder is a big help when exploring the lake.

Most anglers come to Wickiup for the kokanee, but trophy brown trout are the real prize. Wickiup used to hold the record for Oregon's biggest brown and there is a good chance that if the record is ever broken, that fish will come from Wickiup.

The browns feed on kokanee, whitefish and chubs. And they are used to chasing their food. Trollers do well on brown trout when they prospect the old channels and hunt the windward shallows. The best baits are big plastic Smack Baits, Rapalas, A.C. Plugs and similar lures that imitate baitfish. Don't be afraid to use lures that are up to one-third the size of the fish you are chasing. Here the browns average 17 inches and can run to 30 inches or more. A six- to eight-inch lure is not too big.

Kokanee are spread throughout the lake early in the season, but tend to school up and head toward deeper water (the channels) as temperatures warm. Both jigging and trolling are productive throughout the season.

For rainbows, the Davis arm is the best bet. Trolling takes them, and fly-rod tactics can pay off, as well. Small bass can be found in the shallows

At full pool, Wickiup Reservoir covers 10,000 surface acres, making it the largest of the Cascade Lakes. It also produces some of the biggest brown trout.

around the islands and near shoreside structure. Bigger bass can be caught where they find their main food source, minnows, around depth transitions and structure.

Most anglers bring a boat to Wickiup. There are five launches and plenty of campground space to serve the enthusiastic souls braving it out for a big brown or a limit of kokanees on opening day. Bank fishing pays off for trout early in the season. Later in the year, bass and catfish are the main catch from the shoreline.

LOCATION: Deschutes County

BEST TROUT/KOKANEE GEAR-FISHING TECHNIQUES

best	good	slow	Jan	Feb	Mar	Apr	May	Jun	Jul	Aug	Sep	Oct	Nov	Dec
Rainbow						5	4,5,6	4,5,6	4,5,6	4,5,6	4,5,6	4,5,6		
Brown						6	4,8	4,8	4,8	4,8	4,8	4,8		
Kokanee						2,8	2,8	2,8	2,8	2,8	2,8			

1. Spinner and worm troll
2. Kokanee Wedding Ring spinner and corn troll
3. Downrigger lake trout troll
4. Casting Lures: Injured-minnow imitation; spoon; spinner
5. Sliding sinker and jar bait
6. Bobber and bait
7. Spinning-rod fly and bubble
8. Kokanee/trout jigging

BEST BASS AND PANFISH TECHNIQUES

best	good	slow	Jan	Feb	Mar	Apr	May	Jun	Jul	Aug	Sep	Oct	Nov	Dec
Largemouth							1	1,5	5,6	4,6,7	1,2,7	1,2,7		

1. Carolina rig
2. Spinner bait
3. Crappie jig
4. Dropshot
5. Crankbait
6. Top-water plug/buzzbait
7. Senko worm rig

BEST FLY-FISHING TECHNIQUES

best	good	slow	Jan	Feb	Mar	Apr	May	Jun	Jul	Aug	Sep	Oct	Nov	Dec
Rainbow						2	2,5	2,5	2,5	2,5	2,5	2,5		
Brown						2	2,7	2,7	2,7	2,7	2,7	2,7		
Kokanee						5,7	5,7	5,7	5,7	5,7	5,7			

BEST FOR FISHING

April–October

OTHER FAMILY ACTIVITIES

• Sunriver Resort
• Boating
• Swimming
• Hiking
• Wildlife watching
• Picnicking
• Camping
• Hunting
• Birding

1. Two-fly Chironomid and indicator rig
2. Weighted streamer retrieve/ intermediate line leech retrieve
3. Dragonfly/damselfly nymph retrieves
4. Dry-fly dead-drift to rising trout
5. Wind drifting/trolling
6. Dry-fly with dropper nymph/Chironomid
7. Countdown method for sinking fly line

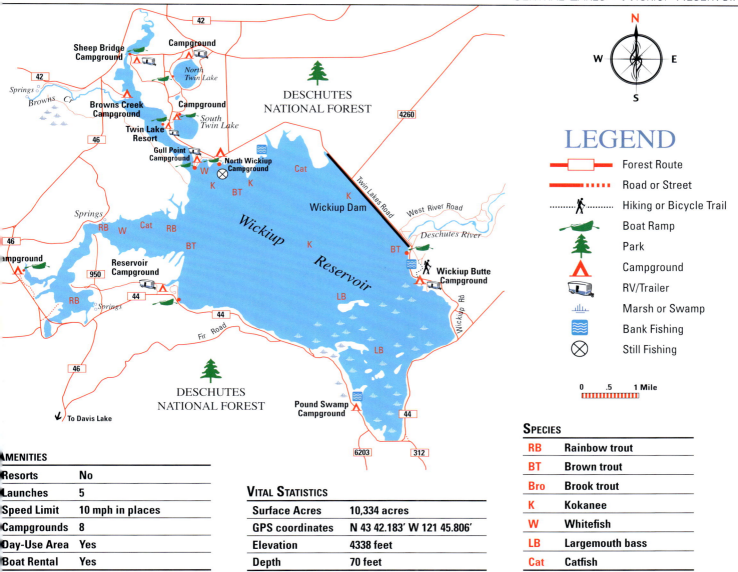

LEGEND

	Forest Route
	Road or Street
	Hiking or Bicycle Trail
	Boat Ramp
	Park
	Campground
	RV/Trailer
	Marsh or Swamp
	Bank Fishing
	Still Fishing

0   .5   1 Mile

SPECIES

RB	Rainbow trout
BT	Brown trout
Bro	Brook trout
K	Kokanee
W	Whitefish
LB	Largemouth bass
Cat	Catfish

AMENITIES

Resorts	No
Launches	5
Speed Limit	10 mph in places
Campgrounds	8
Day-Use Area	Yes
Boat Rental	Yes

VITAL STATISTICS

Surface Acres	10,334 acres
GPS coordinates	N 43 42.183' W 121 45.806'
Elevation	4338 feet
Depth	70 feet

SERVICES

CAMPING & PARKS

- **Deschutes National Forest,** Bend, 97701, (541) 383-5300, www.fs.usda.gov/centraloregon
- **Gull Point Campground,** Info: (541) 383-7869, www.reserveamerica.com
- **Sheep Bridge Campground,** Reserve: (877) 444-6777, www.fs.usda.gov
- **Reservoir Campground,** www.fs.usda.gov
- **North Twin Lake Campground,** (541) 383-5300, www.fs.usda.gov
- **South Twin Lake Campground,** (541) 383-5300, www.fs.usda.gov
- **Cascade Meadows RV Resort,** La Pine, 97739, (541) 536-2244, www.cascademeadowsrvresort.com

ACCOMMODATIONS

- **The Mill Inn B&B,** Bend, 97701, (541) 389-9198, (877) 748-1200, www.millinn.com
- **Lara House B&B,** Bend, 97701, (541) 388-4064, www.larahouse.com
- **Juniper Acres B&B,** Bend, 97701, (541) 389-2193, www.juniperacres.com

TACKLE SHOPS/BOAT RENTALS

- **The Patient Angler Fly Shop,** Bend, 97702, (541) 389-6208, www.patientangler.com
- **Confluence Fly Shop,** Bend, 97702, (541) 678-5633, www.confluenceflyshop.com
- **Wholesale Sports Outdoor Outfitters,** Bend, 97701, (541) 693-5000, (800) 696-0253, www.ca.wholesalesports.com

- **Mickey Finn Guides,** Bend, 97709, (541) 383-3939, www.crane-prairie-resort-guides.com
- **Central Oregon Stillwater Outfitters,** Sunriver, 97707, (541) 598-0008, www.centraloregonfishing.com
- **Fly & Field Outfitters,** Bend, 97702, (866) 800-2812, (541) 318-1616, www.flyandfield.com
- **Sunriver Fly Shop,** Sunriver, 97707, (541) 593-8814, www.sunriverflyshop.com
- **The Hook Fly Shop,** Sunriver, 97707, (888) 230-4665, (541) 593-2358, www.hookfish.com

VISITOR INFORMATION

- **Bend Chamber of Commerce,** Bend, 97701, (541) 382-3221, www.bendchamber.org
- **Sunriver Area Chamber of Commerce,** Sunriver, 97707, (541) 593-8149, www.sunriverchamber.com
- **Atlas of Oregon Lakes,** www.aol.research.pdx.edu
- **Central Oregon Visitors Association,** Bend, 97702, (800) 800-8334, www.visitcentraloregon.com
- **Fishing Central Oregon,** www.fishingcentraloregon.com

NEAREST CITIES/TOWNS

Sunriver, 97707; Bend, 97701; La Pine, 97739

Anthony Lake

Photo by Gary Lewis

A jewel in the Elk Horn Mountains, Anthony Lake (and nearby Mud, Grande Ronde and Black lakes) is heavily stocked by the Oregon Department of Fish and Wildlife when the snow melts in the high country.

This 22-acre lake sits in the alpine shadow of Angel Peak. The Elk Horn Crest Trail runs along one side of the lake. Rainbow trout are the main catch, but there are brook trout in Anthony. Though anglers may catch fish anywhere, the best bank fishing is at either end of the lake. The launch, in shallow water, is suitable for small boats. Some of the best trolling is found where the shallows give way to deeper water straight out from the launch.

All methods work well here, but the fly fisherman operating from a float tube has the advantage when trolling a tandem nymph rig with a slow-sink line.

There may still be snow in June. Plan the trip for July, August or September. Most of Anthony's anglers camp in one of the three nearby campgrounds. Spaces are available first come, first served. Bring mosquito repellent.

From Baker City, go 10 miles northwest on US 30, 14 miles northwest on County Road 1146, then climb 7 miles west on Forest Road 73.

Anthony Lake is the biggest and most popular of this chain of pretty alpine lakes. To avoid the crowds, hike or drive in to one of the other lakes. Remember the mosquito repellent.

LOCATION: Anthony Lake

AMENITIES

Resorts	Anthony Lakes Ski Resort (closed in summer)
Launches	1
Speed Limit	Motors not allowed
Campgrounds	3
Day-Use Area	Yes
Boat Rental	No

VITAL STATISTICS

Surface Acres	22
GPS coordinates	N 44 57.547' W 118 13.752'
Elevation	7131 feet
Depth	10-32 feet

SPECIES

RB	Rainbow trout
Bro	Brook trout

SERVICES

CAMPING & PARKS

- **Anthony Lake Campground,** (541) 523-6391, www.fs.usda.gov
- **Eagles Hot Lake RV Park,** La Grande, 97850, (541) 963-5253, www.eagleshotlakerv.com
- **La Grande Rendezvous RV Park,** La Grande, 97850, (800) 276-6873, (541) 962-0909

ACCOMMODATIONS

- **Hot Lake Springs,** La Grande, 97850, (541) 963-4685, www.hotlakesprings.com
- **A Beaten Path B&B,** Baker City, 97814, (541) 523-9230, www.abeatenpathbb.com
- **Geiser Grand Hotel,** Baker City, 97814, Reserve: (888) 434-7374, (541) 523-1889, www.geisergrand.com

TACKLE SHOPS/BOAT RENTALS

- **Bi-Mart,** La Grande, 97850, (541) 963-2166, www.bimart.com
- **Bi-Mart,** Baker City, 97814, (541) 523-0680, www.bimart.com

VISITOR INFORMATION

- **Baker County Chamber Of Commerce,** Baker City, 97814, (541) 523-5855, www.visitbaker.com
- **Union County Chamber Of Commerce,** La Grande, 97850, (541) 963-8588, www.unioncountychamber.org
- **Wallowa-Whitman National Forest,** Baker City, 97814, (541) 523-6391, www.fs.usda.gov
- **Visit Eastern Oregon,** (800) 332-1843, www.visiteasternoregon.com

NEAREST CITIES/TOWNS

La Grande, 97850; North Powder, 97867; Baker City, 97814

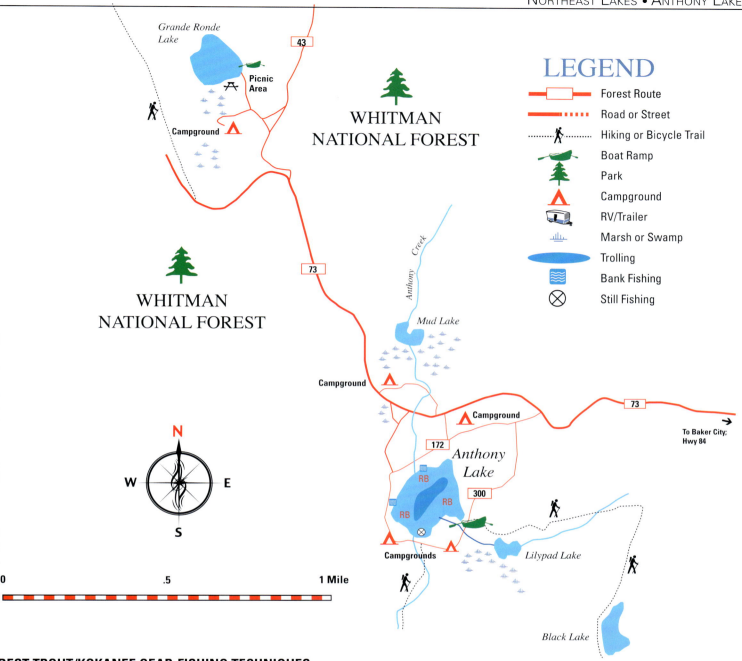

LEGEND

Forest Route	
Road or Street	
Hiking or Bicycle Trail	
Boat Ramp	
Park	
Campground	
RV/Trailer	
Marsh or Swamp	
Trolling	
Bank Fishing	
Still Fishing	

BEST TROUT/KOKANEE GEAR-FISHING TECHNIQUES

best good slow	Jan	Feb	Mar	Apr	May	Jun	Jul	Aug	Sep	Oct	Nov	Dec
Rainbow				5,6	5,6	1,5,6,7	1,5,6,7	1,5,7	1,5,7	5,7		
Brook				5,6	5,6	1,5,6,7	1,5,6,7	1,5,7	1,5,7	5,7		

1. Spinner and worm troll
2. Kokanee Wedding Ring spinner and corn troll
3. Downrigger lake trout troll
4. Casting Lures: Injured-minnow imitation; spoon; spinner
5. Sliding sinker and jar bait
6. Bobber and bait
7. Spinning-rod fly and bubble
8. Kokanee/trout jigging

BEST FLY-FISHING TECHNIQUES

best good slow	Jan	Feb	Mar	Apr	May	Jun	Jul	Aug	Sep	Oct	Nov	Dec
Rainbow				2	2,5	1,3,4,5	1,3,4,5	1,3,4,5	4,5	2,5		
Brook				2	2,5	1,3,4,5	1,3,4,5	1,3,4,5	4,5	2,5		

1. Two-fly Chironomid and indicator rig
2. Weighted streamer retrieve/intermediate line leech retrieve
3. Dragonfly/damselfly nymph retrieves
4. Dry-fly dead-drift to rising trout
5. Wind drifting/trolling
6. Dry-fly with dropper nymph/Chironomid
7. Countdown method for sinking fly line

BEST FOR FISHING
June–October

OTHER FAMILY ACTIVITIES
• Climbing
• Hiking
• Hunting
• Picnicking

Brownlee Reservoir

Follow the Powder River through desert and cowboy country east of Baker City and you'll find Brownlee Reservoir, one of the top warmwater fisheries in the United States. 57 miles long and covering 15,000 surface acres, Brownlee Reservoir is home to bass, crappie, trout, sunfish, catfish and more. It attracts anglers from all over Oregon and Idaho for a chance to tangle with big bass, hatchery trout and slab-sided crappie.

Fishing for smallmouth and largemouth bass picks up as the water warms in March and April. Some of the biggest bass are caught early in the year. Bass take cover up against cover and shoreside structure, while crappie stage in deeper water along drop-offs, but still within easy casting distance of the bank.

Crappie might be the most popular species on this reservoir. Black crappie spawn in early May and white crappie begin to spawn in mid-May. Fishing can be very good in May and June, when bass and crappie can be caught from shore up and down the lake. For bass, try plastic grubs in pumpkin, motor oil and other brownish-green combinations.

Slow-trolling works well on crappie. Run a 1/16-ounce red, yellow or chartreuse jig along cliff walls and riprap or cast to the bank and retrieve. Fly-fishermen can rig for crappie with jigs or small minnow patterns. A crappie tournament is held on the lake in June.

Early in the year, some of the best catfishing is on the upper end of the reservoir, near Farewell Bend. Another great spot for catfish is in flats of the Powder River arm, about a mile upstream from Hewitt Holcomb Park.

Bluegills, pumpkinseed, redear sunfish and perch are easily caught on nightcrawlers or small flies. Prospect for them in and around willows, close to the bank.

In years when winter is cold enough, long enough, ice fishing can be good on the Powder River arm or the upper reservoir.

Boats are available for rent in nearby Richland. Operators bring the boats to the ramp. Tent camping and showers are available at Hewitt Holcomb Park.

LOCATION: Baker County

BEST TROUT/KOKANEE GEAR-FISHING TECHNIQUES

best	good	slow	Jan	Feb	Mar	Apr	May	Jun	Jul	Aug	Sep	Oct	Nov	Dec
Rainbow			1,4,5	1,4,5	1,4,5	1,4,5	1,4,5	1,4,5	1,4,5	1,4,5	1,4,5	1,4,5	1,4,5	1,4,5
Brown			1,4,5	1,4,5	1,4,5	1,4,5	1,4,5	1,4,5	1,4,5	1,4,5	1,4,5	1,4,5	1,4,5	1,4,5

1. Spinner and worm troll
2. Kokanee Wedding Ring spinner and corn troll
3. Downrigger lake trout troll
4. Casting Lures: Injured-minnow imitation; spoon; spinner
5. Sliding sinker and jar bait
6. Bobber and bait
7. Spinning-rod fly and bubble
8. Kokanee/trout jigging

BEST BASS AND PANFISH TECHNIQUES

best	good	slow	Jan	Feb	Mar	Apr	May	Jun	Jul	Aug	Sep	Oct	Nov	Dec
Largemouth			1,3,4	1,3,4	1,3,4	1,3,4	1,2,7	1,4,6	2,5,7	2,6,7	2,6,7	1,2,7	1,3,4	1,3,4
Smallmouth			1,3,4	1,3,4	1,3,4	1,3,4	1,2,7	1,4,6	2,5,7	2,6,7	2,6,7	1,2,7	1,3,4	1,3,4
Crappie			3	3	3	3,4	3,4	3,4	3,4	3,4	3,4	3,4	3	3
Sunfish			3	3	3	3	3	3	3	3	3	3	3	3
Perch			3	3	3	3,4	3,4	3,4	3,4	3,4	3,4	3,4	3	3

1. Carolina rig
2. Spinner bait
3. Crappie jig
4. Dropshot
5. Crankbait
6. Top-water plug/buzzbait
7. Senko worm rig

BEST FLY-FISHING TECHNIQUES

best	good	slow	Jan	Feb	Mar	Apr	May	Jun	Jul	Aug	Sep	Oct	Nov	Dec
Rainbow			5	5	5	5	5	5	5	5	5	5	5	5
Brown			5	5	5	5	5	5	5	5	5	5	5	5
Crappie			2,5	2,5	2,5	2,5	2,5	2,5	2,5	2,5	2,5	2,5	2,5	2,5
Sunfish			1,6	1,6	1,6	1,6	1,6	1,6	1,6	1,6	1,6	1,6	1,6	1,6
Perch			2,5	2,5	2,5	2,5	2,5	2,5	2,5	2,5	2,5	2,5	2,5	2,5

1. Two-fly Chironomid and indicator rig
2. Weighted streamer retrieve/ intermediate line leech retrieve
3. Dragonfly/damselfly nymph retrieves
4. Dry-fly dead-drift to rising trout
5. Wind drifting/trolling
6. Dry-ly with dropper nymph/Chironomid
7. Countdown method for sinking fly line

BEST FOR FISHING

April–October

OTHER FAMILY ACTIVITIES

- Oregon Trail Interpretive Center, www.blm.gov/or/oregontrail/
- Hells Canyon
- Horseback riding
- Huckleberry picking
- Hiking
- Camping
- Boating
- ATV riding
- Snowmobiling
- Birding
- Hunting

Crappie are plentiful and a popular quarry on this large eastern Oregon impoundment.

SPECIES

SB	**Smallmouth bass**
LB	**Largemouth bass**
BCr	**Black crappie**
WC	**White crappie**
BL	**Bluegill**
PS	**Pumpkinseed sunfish**
RS	**Redear sunfish**
CC	**Channel catfish**
FC	**Flathead catfish**
YP	**Yellow perch**
RB	**Rainbow trout**
BT	**Brown trout**
Car	**Carp**
Stu	**Sturgeon (catch and release)**

VITAL STATISTICS

Surface Acres	**15,000**
GPS coordinates	**N 44 46.283' W117 09.142'**
Elevation	**2077 feet**
Depth	**240 feet maximum**

AMENITIES

Resorts	**No**
Launches	**2 in Powder River arm**
Speed Limit	**No**
Campgrounds	**Yes**
Day-Use Area	**Yes**
Boat Rental	**Yes**

SERVICES

CAMPING & PARKS
- **Eagle Valley RV Park,** Richland, 97870, (541) 893-6161, www.facebook.com
- **Hewitt/Holcomb Park,** Richland, 97870, Info: (541) 893-6147, Reserve: (541) 893-6147, www.bakercounty.org
- **Woodhead Park,** (541) 785-3323
- **Halfway Motel & RV Park,** Halfway, 97834, (541) 742-5722, www.halfwaymotel-rvpark.com

ACCOMMODATIONS
- **Pine Valley Lodge,** Halfway, 97834, (541) 742-2027, www.pvlodge.com
- **Clear Creek Inn,** Halfway, 97834, (541) 742-2238, www.clearcreekinn.com

TACKLE SHOPS/BOAT RENTALS
- **York's Park Grocery,** Baker City, 97814, (541) 523-2577
- **Bi-Mart,** Baker City, 97814, (541) 523-0680, www.bimart.com
- **Snake River Rental & Repair,** Richland, 97870, (541) 893-3114
- **Eagle Station,** Richland, 97870, (541) 893-6766
- **Brownlee Charters,** (541) 893-6863, www.brownleecharters.com
- **Hitching Post Store,** Richland, 97870, (541) 893-6176, www.facebook.com

VISITOR INFORMATION
- **Baker County Chamber Of Commerce,** Baker City, 97814, (541) 523-5855, www.visitbaker.com
- **Brownlee Reservoir,** www.brownleereservoir.com
- **Monitor Water Levels,** (water levels can affect launching of boats) www.idahopower.com/ourenvironment/waterinformation/reservoir/default.cfm,
- **Hells Canyon Chamber Of Commerce,** Richland, 97870, (541) 742-4222, www.hellscanyonchamber.com
- **Visit Eastern Oregon,** (800) 332-1843, www.visiteasternoregon.com
- **The Fishing Coaches,** fishingcoaches.org

NEAREST CITIES/TOWNS
Richland, 97870, Baker City, 97814

Wallowa Lake

Photo by Gary Lewis

Wallowa Lake holds the Oregon state record for kokanee. Lake trout and rainbows also grow to large proportion in this rich, deep lake.

Wallowa Lake is the largest natural lake in northeast Oregon. It's home to lake trout, kokanee, bull trout (must be released) and rainbow trout.

This lake, with over 1500 surface acres and an average depth of 160 feet, can be a daunting prospect for the traveling angler. Yet it can be read and the depths plumbed for rainbows, kokanee and big lake trout.

Rainbows are the main catch and most anglers pursue them near the mouth of Wallowa River at the southern end of the lake, where the river takes a hard right turn toward the bank. Most of the trout are hatchery stock that average 10 to 12 inches, but holdover trout can reach 18 inches or more. All methods work here, but fly-fishermen can do very well in the spring in ten feet of water at the mouth of Wallowa River. Try a small, weighted minnow imitation.

Kokanee grow bigger in Wallowa Lake than in most other Oregon waters. Most run between 12 and 18 inches, but it is not uncommon to see a few two-pounders in a 10-fish limit. Wallowa Lake holds United States kokanee record with a 8.23-pound fish caught in 2010.

Favorite kokanee areas are the western shore off Eagle Point and along the eastern bank up and down from the large pine tree. Try jigging for kokanee after ice-off and then switch to trolling in July, August and September. The lake trout (mackinaw) that feed on kokanee can be caught in the shallows after ice-off and again in fall. Jigging and trolling can bring a big mack to the side of the boat.

Boat rentals, launch facilities and ample camping and lodging make this a great destination.

Wallowa Lake can be a good base camp for a hiking or horseback trip into the high country for brook trout and rainbows. For more intimate waters in the Wallowa Valley, take the kids to one of several ponds stocked with catchable rainbows in spring. Try Marr Pond in Enterprise, Victor Pond, west of Wallowa and Wallowa Wildlife Pond for good fishing through the end of June.

AMENITIES

Resorts	Yes
Launches	2
Speed Limit	No
Campgrounds	Yes
Day-Use Area	Yes
Boat Rental	Yes

VITAL STATISTICS

Surface Acres	1508
GPS coordinates	N 45 20.06' W 117 13.15'
Elevation	4383
Depth	299 feet

LOCATION: Wallowa County

BEST TROUT/KOKANEE GEAR-FISHING TECHNIQUES

best good slow	Jan	Feb	Mar	Apr	May	Jun	Jul	Aug	Sep	Oct	Nov	Dec
Rainbow				1,5,6	1,5,6	1,5,6	1,5,6	5,6	5,6	1,5,6		
Kokanee				8	8	2,8	2,8	2	2			
Lake Trout				4	3	3	3	3	3	4		

1. Spinner and worm troll
2. Kokanee Wedding Ring spinner and corn troll
3. Downrigger lake trout troll
4. Casting Lures: Injured-minnow imitation; spoon; spinner
5. Sliding sinker and jar bait
6. Bobber and bait
7. Spinning-rod fly and bubble
8. Kokanee/trout jigging

BEST FLY-FISHING TECHNIQUES

best good slow	Jan	Feb	Mar	Apr	May	Jun	Jul	Aug	Sep	Oct	Nov	Dec
Rainbow				2	2,3,4,5	2,3,4,5	2,3,4,5	1,2,5,7	1,2,5,7	2		
Kokanee				5	5	5	5	5	5	5		
Lake Trout				2	2	7	7	7	7	2		

1. Two-fly Chironomid and indicator rig
2. Weighted streamer retrieve/ intermediate line leech retrieve
3. Dragonfly/damselfly nymph retrieves
4. Dry-fly dead-drift to rising trout
5. Wind drifting/trolling
6. Dry-ly with dropper nymph/Chironomid
7. Countdown method for sinking fly line

BEST FOR FISHING

April–October

OTHER FAMILY ACTIVITIES

- Hells Canyon Mule Days, www.hellscanyonmuledays.com
- Wallowa Lake Tramway, www.wallowalaketramway.com
- Eagle Cap Excursion Train, www.eaglecaptrain.com
- Chief Joseph Days, www.chiefjosephdays.com
- Art galleries, www.josephoregonartists.com
- Chief Joseph Memorial
- Camping
- Mini golf
- Shopping
- Go-carts
- Wildlife watching
- Hiking
- Horseback riding
- Boating

SPECIES

RB	**Rainbow trout**
LT	**Lake trout**
K	**Kokanee**
Bul	**Bull trout (endangered)**

LEGEND

	State Route
	Road or Street
	Hiking or Bicycle Trail
	Boat Ramp
	Park
	Campground
	RV/Trailer
	Trolling
	Bank Fishing
	Still Fishing

0 · .5 · 1 Mile

SERVICES

CAMPING & PARKS

- **Wallowa Lake State Park,** Joseph, 97846, (541) 432-8855, www.reserveamerica.com
- **Wallowa Lake County Park,** day-use only, (541) 426-3332, www.wallowalake.net
- **Wallowa Lake Marina,** Joseph, 97846, (541) 432-9115. www.wallowalakemarina.com
- **Wallowa Lake Lodge,** Joseph, 97846, (541) 432-9821, www.wallowalake.com
- **Wallowa Lake Vacation Rentals,** (800) 709-2039, www.wallowalakevacationrentals.com
- **Park At the River,** Joseph, 97846, (541) 432-8800, www.parkattheriver.com

ACCOMMODATIONS

- **The Bronze Antler B&B,** Joseph, 97846, (541) 432-0230, www.bronzeantler.com
- **Creekside Country Haven,** Joseph, 97846, (541) 263-0288, www.creeksidecountryhaven.com

TACKLE SHOPS/BOAT RENTALS

- **Joseph Fly Shoppe,** Joseph, 97846, (541) 432-4343, josephflyshoppe.com
- **Sports Corral,** Joseph, 97846, (541) 432-4363, www.facebook.com
- **Ninebark Outfitters,** Joseph, 97846, (541) 426-4855, www.ninebarkoutfitters.com
- **Tri-State Outfitters,** Enterprise, 97828, (541) 426-4468, www.tri-stateoutfitters.com
- **Winding Waters River Expeditions,** Joseph, 97846, (877) 426-7238, (541) 432-0747, www.windingwatersrafting.com
- **Eagle Cap Fishing Guides,** (800) 940-3688

VISITOR INFORMATION

- **Joseph Chamber of Commerce,** Joseph, 97846, (541) 432-0338, www.josephoregon.com
- **Wallowa County Chamber of Commerce,** Enterprise, 97828, (541) 426-4622, www.wallowacountychamber.com
- **City of Joseph,** Joseph, 97846, (541) 432-3832, www.josephoregon.org
- **Wallowa-Whitman National Forest,** Baker City, 97814, (541) 523-6391, www.fs.usda.gov/wallowa-whitman
- **Visit Eastern Oregon,** (800) 332-1843, www.visiteasternoregon.com

NEAREST CITIES/TOWNS

Joseph, 97846; Enterprise, 97828

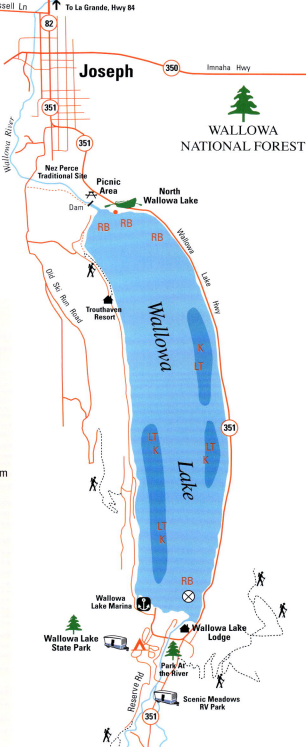

Willow Creek Lake

Willow Creek gathers her water from the Blue Mountains and runs them down to the Columbia. A reservoir, built to control periodic flooding of the town of Heppner, Willow Creek Lake, is located less than a mile upstream from Heppner.

The 156-acre impoundment draws anglers from nearby Hermiston and other towns to do battle with its piscine inhabitants. Bass, crappie and catfish are the mainstays. April, May and June are the best months for rainbow trout.

Oregon Department of Fish and Wildlife stocks the lake with rainbow trout in May and June. Trout put on weight fast in this food-rich water. Most anglers opt for a bobber and worm or PowerBait to put fish on the stringer, but spinners, trolling and fly-fishing techniques are productive.

The best trout water is along the rip-rapped south bank and across the lake along the north shore. The water drops off quickly to a maximum depth of 85 feet at the dam.

When the water warms in spring, crappie fishing turns on. This is a great time to introduce a youngster to the sport. Bait works well, but serious crappie anglers should opt for plastic grubs and tiny minnow imitations. Fly fishermen can boat a lot of fish here. Crappie are the most abundant fish in the lake—to the point that they appear to be stunted. Anglers should keep all crappie they catch.

Brown bullhead catfish are abundant and can be caught all day long, but the best fishing for catfish is in the low light of morning or evening.

Access is easiest along the south bank. A day park overlooks the lake. A paved boat ramp with ample trailer parking makes it convenient to launch a boat. Bank anglers prefer Willow Creek Lake fishing access which opens at 4 a.m. and closes at 10 p.m. For camping, Willow Creek Campground offers RV hookups, a great view and showers.

LOCATION: Morrow County

BEST BASS AND PANFISH TECHNIQUES

best good slow	Jan	Feb	Mar	Apr	May	Jun	Jul	Aug	Sep	Oct	Nov	Dec
Largemouth				1	1	1,6,7	1,6,7	1,6,7	2,5	2,5		
Smallmouth				1	1	1,6,7	1,6,7	1,6,7	2,5	2,5		
Crappie			3	3	3	3	3	3	3	3		
Bluegill			3	3	3	3	3	3	3	3		

1. Carolina rig
2. Spinner bait
3. Crappie jig
4. Dropshot
5. Crankbait
6. Top-water plug/buzzbait
7. Senko worm rig

BEST TROUT/KOKANEE GEAR-FISHING TECHNIQUES

best good slow	Jan	Feb	Mar	Apr	May	Jun	Jul	Aug	Sep	Oct	Nov	Dec
Rainbow	5	5	1,4,5	1,4,5	1,4,5,7	1,4,5,7	1,4,5,7	1,4,5,7	1,4,5	1,4,5	5	5

1. Spinner and worm troll
2. Kokanee Wedding Ring spinner and corn troll
3. Downrigger lake trout troll
4. Casting Lures: Injured-minnow imitation; spoon; spinner
5. Sliding sinker and jar bait
6. Bobber and bait
7. Spinning-rod fly and bubble
8. Kokanee/trout jigging

AMENITIES

Resorts	No
Launches	Yes
Speed Limit	10mph
Campgrounds	Yes

SERVICES

CAMPING & PARKS
- **Willow Creek RV Park**, (541) 676-5576, www.willowcreekparkdistrict.com
- **Northwestern Motel & RV Park**, Heppner, 97836, (541) 676-9167, www.heppnerlodging.com

- **ACCOMMODATIONS**
- **Woolery House B&B**, Ione, 97843, (541) 422-7218, www.merchantcircle.com

TACKLE SHOPS/BOAT RENTALS
- **Pettyjohn's Farm & Builders Supply**, Heppner, 97836, (541) 676-9157, www.facebook.com

- **VISITOR INFORMATION**
- **Heppner Chamber of Commerce**, Heppner, 97836, (541) 676-5536, www.heppnerchamber.com
- **Eastern Oregon Visitors Association**, (800) 332-1843, www.visiteasternoregon.com
- **Southern Oregon Visitors Association**, www.southernoregon.org

NEAREST CITIES/TOWNS
Heppner, 97836

VITAL STATISTICS

Surface Acres	156
GPS coordinates	N45 20.472' W 119 31.673'
Elevation	2065
Depth	85 feet

SPECIES

RB	Rainbow trout
LB	Largemouth bass
SB	Smallmouth bass
Cr	Crappie
PS	Pumpkinseed sunfish
Cat	Catfish

BEST FOR FISHING

March–June

OTHER FAMILY ACTIVITIES

• Museum
• Bowling
• Swimming
• Fair and rodeo (in August)
• Hike Oregon Trail
• Willow Creek Symphony

Marc Ladyga of Bend fished Willow Creek Lake in early June to put the graphite to this nice trout. For hatchery rainbows, April, May and June are the best months. When the water warms, crappie, sunfish and bass become more active.

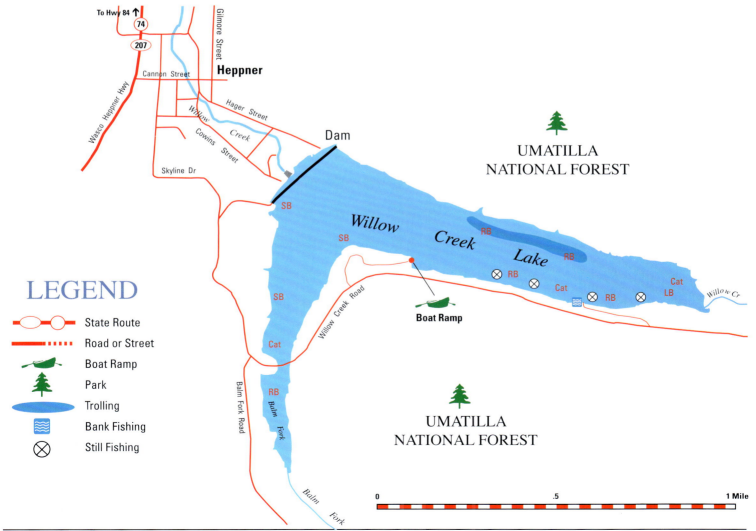

LEGEND

State Route

Road or Street

Boat Ramp

Park

Trolling

Bank Fishing

Still Fishing

Agency/Upper Klamath Lakes

Photo by Gary Lewis

Agency and Upper Klamath lakes are home to some of Oregon's biggest rainbows. An average trout here runs 18 to 20 inches. A big one can tip the scales to 10 pounds or more.

R ed-winged blackbirds fly back and forth from their nests in the willows. Grebes plunge underwater, searching for minnows or fleeing from the boat. White pelicans wheel on the breeze, black wingtips dark against the sky.

Upper Klamath and Agency lakes grow some of the biggest trout in Oregon. It's big water. Maybe that's why it doesn't get much pressure. Shallow waters, good insect production, and lots of baitfish produce large rainbows.

Three- to five-pound rainbows are standard fare for anglers on Upper Klamath and Agency lakes, but those who put their time in on the water will often catch much larger fish. Every year a few anglers boat big rainbows weighing in the high-teens.

When you go, because go you must, if you hunt big trout, take six-pound-test line, tinted green to blend with the color of the water. Fish Little Cleo

spoons or minnow-imitating plugs that resemble chubs or perch. Casting allows the angler to fish more water as the boat drifts with the wind.

Minnow imitations, such as jerkbaits and swimbaits, and in-line spinners are also good choices. Don't troll in a straight line. Make S-turns along your course, to make your minnow imitation change directions suddenly, diving and climbing in the water column, just like a baitfish being pursued by a predator. Such direction changes trigger strikes.

Multiple in-line spinner blades create action and vibration that can pay off in deeper water. The flash simulates a school of baitfish and draws the attention of your quarry. A similar effect can be achieved with artificial bait that leaves a trail of sparkles. The sparkles suggest tiny fish scales which trigger feeding instincts in larger fish.

For fly-rod action, Upper Klamath and Agency are hard to beat. The key is mobility. An angler needs to stay on the move until the fish are located. Best to do that with a shallow-running boat and a motor, rather than a float tube and fins.

Chironomids, snails, damselflies, crayfish and minnows are all on the menu, but many fly-rodders opt for leeches on these waters. Presentation is everything.

Good action can be found in the tules along the shore, especially in and around the mouths of feeder streams like the Wood River and the Williamson. Sometimes you can see the tules shake as the fish bash their way through. Cast right to the edge of the reeds, let the fly sink, then start the retrieve with one-inch strips punctuated by pauses to let the fly sink.

Bank fishermen do well in the area around Pelican Marina, north of Hagelstein Park, and at the mouth of the Wood River. Brown spinners and plugs in a chub, perch, or rainbow pattern are good bets for spin-fishermen.

In the spring, boaters fish the shoreline in Wocus Bay, along Eagle Ridge and in Shoalwater Bay. Troll bait, or minnow-imitating spinners, plugs or spoons on a long line. Eight feet is the average depth, with a few spots going as deep as 25 feet. Angling is open year-round with a bag limit of one trout per day.

UPPER KLAMATH LAKE VITAL STATISTICS

Surface Acres	61,543
Elevation	4139 feet
Depth	50 feet, 8 feet average

AGENCY LAKE VITAL STATISTICS

Surface Acres	9,298
Elevation	4139 feet
Depth	10 feet

SPECIES

RB	Rainbow trout
YP	Yellow perch

BEST TROUT/KOKANEE GEAR-FISHING TECHNIQUES

best	good	slow	Jan	Feb	Mar	Apr	May	Jun	Jul	Aug	Sep	Oct	Nov	Dec
Rainbow			5	5	5	1,5	1,4,5	4	4	4	4	1,4,5	5	5

1. Spinner and worm troll
2. Kokanee Wedding Ring spinner and corn troll
3. Downrigger lake trout troll
4. Casting Lures: Injured-minnow imitation; spoon; spinner
5. Sliding sinker and jar bait
6. Bobber and bait
7. Spinning-rod fly and bubble
8. Kokanee/trout jigging

BEST FLY-FISHING TECHNIQUES

best	good	slow	Jan	Feb	Mar	Apr	May	Jun	Jul	Aug	Sep	Oct	Nov	Dec
Rainbow			2	2	2	2,5	2,3,5	2,3,5	2,3,7	2,3,7	2,3,7	2,3,5	2	2

1. Two-fly Chironomid and indicator rig
2. Weighted streamer retrieve/intermediate line leech retrieve
3. Dragonfly/damselfly nymph retrieves
4. Dry-fly dead-drift to rising trout
5. Wind drifting/trolling
6. Dry-fly with dropper nymph/Chironomid
7. Countdown method for sinking fly line

BEST FOR FISHING

April–June
September–October

OTHER FAMILY ACTIVITIES

- Crater Lake National Park
- Lava Beds National Monument
- Favell Museum
- Ross Ragland Theater
- Running Y Resort
- Waterfowl hunting
- Parks
- Hiking
- Birding
- Camping
- Canoe trails

SERVICES

CAMPING & PARKS

- **Crater Lake National Park,** Crater Lake, 97604, (541) 594-3000, www.nps.gov/crla
- **Fremont-Winema National Forest,** Klamath, 97601, (541) 883-6714, www.fs.usda.gov/fremont-winema
- **Rocky Point Resort,** Klamath Falls, 97601, (541) 356-2287, www.rockypointoregon.com
- **Agency Lake Resort,** Chiloquin, 97624, (541) 783-2489, www.agencylakeresort.net
- **Klamath Falls KOA,** Klamath Falls, 97603, Reserve: (800) 562-9036, (541) 884-4644, www.koa.com/campgrounds/klamath
- **Oregon Motel 8 & RV Park,** Klamath Falls, 97601, (541) 883-3431, www.oregonmotel8rvpark.com
- **Tingley Lake Estates,** Klamath Falls, 97603, (541) 882-8386, www.facebook.com

ACCOMMODATIONS

- **Lonesome Duck,** Chiloquin, 97624, (541) 783-2783, www.lonesomeduck.com
- **Lodge at Running Y Ranch,** Klamath Falls, 97601, Info: (541) 850-5500, Reserve: (800) 569-0029, www.runningy.com
- **Lake of the Woods Resort,** Klamath Falls, 97601, (866) 201-4194, (541) 883-6714, www.lakeofthewoodsresort.com

TACKLE SHOPS/BOAT RENTALS

- **The Ledge,** Klamath Falls, 97601, (541) 882-5586, www.theledgeoutdoorstore.com
- **Parker's Rod & Gun Rack,** Klamath Falls, 97603, (541) 883-3726, www.yelp.com
- **Roe Outfitters,** Klamath Falls, 97603, (541) 884-3825, www.roeoutfitters.com
- **Trophy Troutfitters/Brent Hublitz,** Klamath Falls, 97603, (541) 591-6221, www.trophytroutfitters.com

VISITOR INFORMATION

- **Klamath County Chamber Of Commerce,** Klamath Falls, 97601, (877) 552-6284, (541) 884-5193, www.klamath.org
- **Discover Klamath Visitor & Convention Bureau,** Klamath Falls, 97601, (800) 445-6728, (541) 882-1501, www.2chambers.com
- **Southern Oregon Visitors Association,** www.southernoregon.org

NEAREST CITIES/TOWNS

Klamath Falls, 97601; Chiloquin, 97624

LOCATION: Klamath County

LEGEND

	US Highway
	State Route
	Forest Route
	Road or Street
	Hiking or Bicycle Trail
	Boat Ramp
	Park
	Campground
	RV/Trailer
	Marsh or Swamp
	Trolling
	Bank Fishing

0   .5   1 Mile

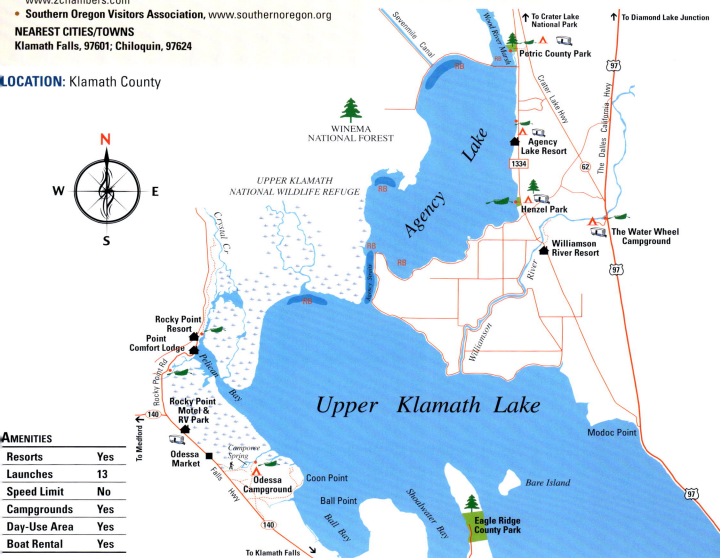

AMENITIES

Resorts	Yes
Launches	13
Speed Limit	No
Campgrounds	Yes
Day-Use Area	Yes
Boat Rental	Yes

Krumbo Reservoir

A shallow lake on the west side of the Steens Mountains, Krumbo Reservoir is a great rainbow and largemouth bass lake in the desert. And it is a great choice in March and early April, before the trout in most other waters have snapped out of their winter torpor.

Best bet is to bring a float tube, canoe or car-topper. But there is bank access. Anglers can fish at the dam or walk from the ramp to one of two rocky points that look out over some of the lake's deeper water. Fish a sliding sinker and 48 inches of leader terminating at a No. 14-16 treble hook with Power Bait or Gulp!

With a boat, launch at the ramp and fish out from the cove to 15 yards from the rocky point on the south. A long weedbed stretches north across the lake. The lake averages ten feet deep. Rainbows stack along the weeds and grow fat on Callibaetis and Chironomids.

Use a clear intermediate sinking line and troll along the weedbed. Fish a No. 12-14 Callibaetis nymph, or better yet, a pair of them. To tempt with Chironomids, employ No. 16-18 zebra, black or red midge larva imitations under an indicator.

Leech patterns are effective here as well. Use black, red or olive Buggers, weighted at the head. Twitch the fly with one-inch pulls.

Krumbo is stocked throughout the early season. Trout that winter-over grow to 16 inches in their second year. Every season the lake produces a number of 20-inch and bigger fish.

This lake can produce big largemouth. In early morning or late evening, cast fly-rod poppers to the shoreside reeds. Stay on the move. Bass come into the shallows to feed in low light. Spin-fishermen can pop big bass by cranking shallow-running crankbaits or spinnerbaits. During the day, go deep near rocky points where largemouth ambush their feed.

Covered tables are provided. A restroom can be found near the dam and at the boat ramp. A handicap-accessible fishing platform is near the boat ramp. The launch is paved with a nice dock. Electric motors are permitted.

Krumbo is open for day-use-only from the opening of trout season through October 31. An automatic gate that opens 30 minutes before sunrise and closes 30 minutes after sunset.

Page Springs campground can be found a few miles down the road. There is RV camping available in private campgrounds on both sides of the Malheur National Wildlife Refuge.

Bass action heats up as the water warms, but Krumbo can be a good bet for an early season road trip for rainbow trout.

LOCATION: Krumbo Reservoir

BEST TROUT/KOKANEE GEAR-FISHING TECHNIQUES

best	good	slow	Jan	Feb	Mar	Apr	May	Jun	Jul	Aug	Sep	Oct	Nov	Dec
Rainbow						5,6,7	5,6,7	5,6	5,6	5,6	5,6,7	5,6,7		

1. Spinner and worm troll
2. Kokanee Wedding Ring spinner and corn troll
3. Downrigger lake trout troll
4. Casting Lures: Injured-minnow imitation; spoon; spinner
5. Sliding sinker and jar bait
6. Bobber and bait
7. Spinning-rod fly and bubble
8. Kokanee/trout jigging

BEST FLY-FISHING TECHNIQUES

best	good	slow	Jan	Feb	Mar	Apr	May	Jun	Jul	Aug	Sep	Oct	Nov	Dec
Rainbow						1,2,3	1,2,3	1,2,3,4	1	1	1,2	1,2,3		

1. Two-fly Chironomid and indicator rig
2. Weighted streamer retrieve/intermediate line leech retrieve
3. Dragonfly/damselfly nymph retrieves
4. Dry-fly dead-drift to rising trout
5. Wind drifting/trolling
6. Dry-fly with dropper nymph/Chironomid
7. Countdown method for sinking fly line

BEST FOR FISHING

March–May

OTHER FAMILY ACTIVITIES

- Hiking
- Historic Frenchglen
- Buena Vista Viewpoint
- Steens Mountain Loop
- Indian petroglyphs
- Malheur National Wildlife Refuge
- Wildlife viewing
- Crystal Crane Hot Springs

LEGEND

▬▬▪▪▪	Road or Street
🚣	Boat Ramp
⏚	Marsh or Swamp
⬮	Trolling
〰	Bank Fishing

MALHEUR NATIONAL
WILDLIFE REFUGE

Krumbo Reservoir

Dam

Krumbo Creek

Reservoir Road

Krumbo

To Hwy 205, Burns

Dry Krumbo Creek

Krumbo Creek

```
0            .5           1 Mile
```

N
W E
S

SERVICES

CAMPING & PARKS
- **Crystal Crane Hot Springs,** Burns, 97720, (541) 493-2312, www.cranehotsprings.com
- **The Narrows RV Park,** Princeton, 97721, (541) 495-2006, (800) 403-3294, www.narrowsrvpark.com
- **Page Springs Campground,** Frenchglen, 97736, Info: (541) 573-4400, www.blm.gov

ACCOMMODATIONS
- **Frenchglen Hotel State Heritage Site,** Frenchglen, 97736, (541) 493-2825, www.facebook.com
- **Steens Mountain Wilderness Resort,** Frenchglen, 97736, Reserve: (800) 542-3765, (541) 493-2415, www.steensmountainresort.com

TACKLE SHOPS/BOAT RENTALS
- **Kiger Creek Fly Shop,** Hines, 97738, (541) 573-1329

VISITOR INFORMATION
- **Harney County Chamber of Commerce,** Burns, 97720, (541) 573-2636, www.harneycounty.com
- **Malheur National Wildlife Refuge,** Princeton, 97721, (541) 493-2612, www.fws.gov/malheur
- **Round Barn Visitor Center,** Diamond, 97722, (888) 493-2420, (541) 493-2070, www.roundbarn.net
- **Hart Mountain National Antelope Refuge,** Lakeview, 97630, (541) 947-2731, www.fws.gov
- **Alvord Desert,** www.blm.gov
- **Steens Mountain,** www.blm.gov
- **Southern Oregon Visitors Association,** www.southernoregon.org

NEAREST CITIES/TOWNS
Frenchglen, 97736

AMENITIES

Resorts	No
Launches	Yes
Speed Limit	Electric motors allowed
Campgrounds	No
Day-Use Area	Yes

VITAL STATISTICS

Surface Acres	150
GPS coordinates	N42 57.062' W 118 48.415'
Elevation	4194
Depth	16 feet

BEST BASS AND PANFISH TECHNIQUES

best	good	slow	Jan	Feb	Mar	Apr	May	Jun	Jul	Aug	Sep	Oct	Nov	Dec
Largemouth						1	1,6	1,6	1,6	1,6	1,2	1,2		

1. **Carolina rig**
2. **Spinner bait**
3. **Crappie jig**
4. **Dropshot**
5. **Crankbait**
6. **Top-water plug/buzzbait**
7. **Senko worm rig**

SPECIES

RB	Rainbow trout
LB	Largemouth bass

Owyhee Reservoir

Owyhee Reservoir is named for the river, which was named for the old spelling of Hawaii. Two Hawaiian islanders were killed by Indians near the river in 1819. Peter Skene Ogden, who explored the region in the early 1800s, named the river in their honor.

The 52-mile reservoir, with 150 miles of shoreline, is the largest in the state. The 417-foot dam was constructed in the late 1920s and finished in 1932 by the U.S. Bureau of Reclamation. The project furnishes water for 105,249 acres of farm and ranchland.

For the fisherman, Owyhee Reservoir is a lake rich in opportunity and room to roam. Chiseled by wind and water, the landscape is a rock garden of pinnacles, rimrock and flat-topped buttes. The sculptured scenery above the water is indicative of the structure below the surface that holds largemouth, smallmouth, crappie, catfish and trout.

Rock walls, shelves, boulders, channels, slides, islands and underwater humps hold bass and crappie. Early in the year, the best largemouth fishing is in the coves and around the hot springs. Later, bass migrate out to roam the main reservoir. Smallmouth bass may be found anywhere in the lake, but the top end seems to hold the highest numbers.

For crappie, employ a chartreuse or red-and-white-skirted crappie jig, tipped with a Crappie Nibble for extra color and scent. For faster action, rig with two jigs.

Owyhee's catfish are channels, blues and brown bullheads. Use a sliding sinker rig anywhere in the lake in mud flats in about 10 to 15 feet of water and you will catch them, but the biggest fish (up to 30 pounds) are reported to come from the top of the reservoir. The best baits include nightcrawlers, chicken liver, mackerel or cut crappie.

Trout don't get much attention at Owyhee Reservoir, but the fishing can be good, especially in years that follow higher water cycles. Most of the rainbows are caught in the area between the dam and Dry Creek. The best bet is to wind-drift with a sliding sinker rig and a jar bait.

The canyon's beauty may be perilous to the boater. Water levels fluctuate over the course of the year and danger can lurk just beneath the surface. Submerged islands and rock spires can break a prop or gash a hull when the water goes from 100 feet deep to 10 feet to 10 inches to nothing.

There is a mercury advisory for the lake. Consider releasing the larger fish that may have high mercury buildup in their bodies. Younger, smaller fish should be safe to eat.

The lake is popular with waterfowlers. Upland bird hunters pursue chukar, quail and pheasants in the surrounding hills and canyons. Wild horses, bighorn sheep and mule deer may be seen on the hills above the water.

LOCATION: Malheur County

SERVICES

CAMPING & PARKS
- **Indian Creek Campground,** (800) 551-6949, Reserve: (800) 452-5687, www.oregonstateparks.org
- **McCormack Campground,** (800) 551-6949, Reserve: (800) 452-5687, www.oregonstateparks.org
- **Vale Trails RV Park,** (541) 473-3879, www.valetrailsrvpark.com
- **Lake Owyhee State Park,** Reserve: Reserve: (800) 452-5687, (541) 339-2331, www.reserveamerica.com
- **Gordon Gulch Ramp,** day-use only, Reserve: (800) 452-5687, (541) 869-2365, www.boatescape.com
- **Leslie Gulch,** (541) 473-3144, www.blm.gov
- **Owyhee Reservoir Boat Ramp,** (800) 551-6949, www.recreation.gov
- **Lake Owyhee Resort,** Adrian, 97991, (541) 339-2331, www.boatescape.com

ACCOMMODATIONS
- **Oregon Trail Inn B&B,** Vale, 97918, (541) 473-3030, www.searshomebb.com
- **Virtue House B&B,** Ontario, 97914, (541) 889-1996, www.virtuehouse.com

TACKLE SHOPS/BOAT RENTALS
- **Malheur Drug Store,** Vale, 97918, (541) 473-3333

VISITOR INFORMATION
- **Vale Chamber Of Commerce,** Vale, 97918, (541) 473-3800, www.valechamber.com
- **Ontario Chamber Of Commerce,** Ontario, 97914, (866) 989-8012, (541) 889-8012, www.ontariochamber.com
- **Southern Oregon Visitors Association,** www.southernoregon.org
- **Eastern Oregon Visitors Association,** (800) 332-1843, www.visiteasternoregon.com

NEAREST CITIES/TOWNS
Vale, 97918; Nyssa, 97913; Ontario, 97914

BEST FLY-FISHING TECHNIQUES

best good slow	Jan	Feb	Mar	Apr	May	Jun	Jul	Aug	Sep	Oct	Nov	Dec
Rainbow	2,5	2,5	2,5	2,5	2,4,5	2,5,7	2,5,7	2,5,7	2,5,7	2,4,5	2,5	2,5
Crappie	2	2	2	2	2	2	2	2	2	2	2	2
Bass	2	2	2	2	2	2	2	2	2	2	2	2

1. Two-fly Chironomid and indicator rig
2. Weighted streamer retrieve/intermediate line leech retrieve
3. Dragonfly/damselfly nymph retrieves
4. Dry-fly dead-drift to rising trout
5. Wind drifting/trolling
6. Dry-fly with dropper nymph/Chironomid
7. Countdown method for sinking fly line

BEST TROUT/KOKANEE GEAR-FISHING TECHNIQUES

best good slow	Jan	Feb	Mar	Apr	May	Jun	Jul	Aug	Sep	Oct	Nov	Dec
Rainbow	1,5	1,5	1,5	1,5	1,5	1,5	5	5	1,5	1,5	1,5	1,5

1. Spinner and worm troll
2. Kokanee Wedding Ring spinner and corn troll
3. Downrigger lake trout troll
4. Casting Lures: Injured-minnow imitation; spoon; spinner
5. Sliding sinker and jar bait
6. Bobber and bait
7. Spinning-rod fly and bubble
8. Kokanee/trout jigging

BEST FOR FISHING
April–October

OTHER FAMILY ACTIVITIES
- Four River Cultural Center and Museum
- Hunting
- Hiking
- Rafting
- Biking
- Picnicking
- Swimming
- Hot Springs
- Birding

This huge reservoir in southeast Oregon is worth the effort it takes to get to this remote corner of the state. But bring a boat if you plan on fishing. There is plenty of public-land bank access, but few roads.

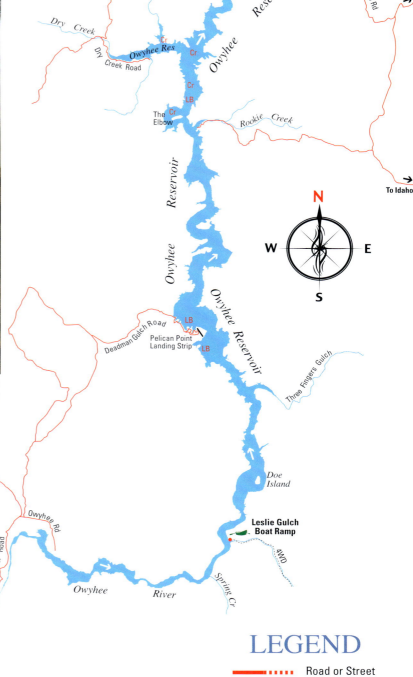

AMENITIES

Resorts	Yes
Launches	5
Speed Limit	No
Campgrounds	5
Day-Use Area	Yes
Boat Rental	Yes

SPECIES

SB	Smallmouth bass
Cr	Crappie
CC	Channel catfish
YP	Yellow perch
RB	Rainbow trout

VITAL STATISTICS

Surface Acres	13,900
GPS coordinates	N 43 36.640' W 117 15.612'
Elevation	2670
Depth	117 feet

BEST BASS AND PANFISH TECHNIQUES

best good slow	Jan	Feb	Mar	Apr	May	Jun	Jul	Aug	Sep	Oct	Nov	Dec
Largemouth	3,4	3,4	3,4,7	3,4,7	1,2,7	1,2,7	5,6,7	5,6,7	5,6,7	1,5,7	3,4	3,4
Smallmouth	3,4	3,4	3,4,7	3,4,7	2,5	2,5,7	5,6,7	5,6,7	5,7	5,7	3,4	3,4
Crappie	3	3	3	3	3	3	3	3	3	3	3	3

1. Carolina rig
2. Spinner bait
3. Crappie jig
4. Dropshot
5. Crankbait
6. Top-water plug/buzzbait
7. Senko worm rig

LEGEND

······	Road or Street
	Boat Ramp
	Park
	Campground
	RV/Trailer

0   1 Mile